Mind The Mem

Learn To Memorize Anything

By Scott Hughey

Copyright

Dedication

This one's for the girls. Emma and Sarah, I love you. Hopefully you'll never forget that.

Acknowledgements

Thanks to CC Dowling for editing this manuscript for me. Any errors in this book are mine, and not hers. Also, the images in this book only exist because she insisted I add them.

Thanks to Joy, for encouraging me to write a non-fiction book.

Thanks to my boss, despite what I say later in the book.

Join My Reader List For Freebies

I hope you enjoy this story as much as I did writing it. If so, why not leave an Amazon review to help others find it? You can do so here.

http://amzn.to/2icnaRr

And also, be sure to sign up for my reader's group at

www.TheWriteScott.com

Members receive free stories for signing up, and get notified about upcoming books.

Contents

1. Shall We Play A Game?

Hi. You're reading the beginning of this book, so I can safely assume you're interested in improving your memory. Good for you. Maybe you want to know how to stop forgetting people's names, or how to memorize an entire deck of cards. Or maybe you're my mom, and you're reading this because you feel like you have to.

I'm kidding. I'm reasonable sure my mom's never read any of my books. (Um, hi, Mom. If you're seeing this now, then obviously I'm kidding.)

I'm glad you're here. We're going to go on a few journeys together. In fact, that's exactly what it feels like to remember things the way I'll teach you. It's like taking a really odd trip inside your mind. Along the way, you'll see images like rabbits taking pictures of statues. The best thing? None of this is medically induced.

It's super easy to remember things like that, and also a bit fun.

I'll be showing some of my journeys, and the path I took to a memory that's changing my life. More importantly, you'll be finding the way to your own path.

That's the key. The path has to belong to you, or it will never work. I can't let you into my Memory Palaces, but I can help you make your own. (I really want to call it a Mind Palace, but some of the purists will object to the term. "That's pure fiction," they'll say, "right out of Sherlock. Call it a *Memory Palace*, if you must. Better yet, call it the *Method of Loci*.")

I guess they're right. More importantly, if I talk about Mind Palaces here, and someone researches them, they'll learn more about the BBC show, Sherlock than memory. So it's a Memory Palace. But, secretly, to myself, I call it the other thing. Mind Palace sounds cooler. If it was good enough for Stephen Moffat, one of the greatest entertainment writers of our time, then it's good enough for me.

Less than 400 words in, and already I'm side-tracked. I'll remember to do better.

Enough of the introduction. Let's start.

The Game

First off, we're about to do an exercise. The tendency might be to just read, but that's cheating yourself. You'll find that following along, rather than just reading the words, will open your mind without the hassle of brain surgery. You'll be amazed at how smart you feel. Well, that is, unless you're already a memory champion. And if you are, how awesome is that? Ladies and Gentlemen, actual memory champions are reading my book on improving their memory! Thanks for the endorsement.

Right. Let's start again. For realsies this time.

Picture a room you're so familiar with, you can close your eyes and see where everything is. For now, we're going to keep it simple. Maybe you're imagining your childhood home. A college dorm room. The kitchen from the house you currently live.

It can be anywhere, as long as you can see it in your mind's eye. Now pinpoint ten locations in the area. These are places like the couch, a lamp, or that recliner that needs throwing out.

You're going to find a path from one of these locations to the next. Unless the room calls for a different progression, I typically start in the doorway, and go clockwise until I get all the way around.

Eventually, you'll move from room to room, but for now, the path won't stray from this first room. Make sure you know where everything is, and make the path a logical progression through the room. This is the same way you'll take every time you use this room. As much as possible, don't backtrack or cross your path.

It's like the original Ghostbusters, when Spengler said, "Don't cross the streams." Why? "It would be bad."

If you're fuzzy on the whole good/bad thing, then here's a better reason. Momentarily, we'll be picturing wild images in these places. If you cross your path, it confuses the mind. Did you put the gremlin in the window, or was it by the stairs?

To recap, we're making a logical path through a room, finding ten locations that we'll visualize later. To demonstrate, I'm going to use my living room. Remember to find ten locations for yourself.

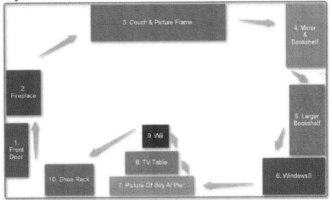

One: I open the front door, and the bells on the window blinds jingle.

Two: Immediately to my left is the fireplace. There's a marble floor right in front of it.

Three: Here's a couch on the left wall. Above it is a picture frame.

Four: A mirror, with a small bookshelf beneath it, sits adjacent to the couch. I'm not going into any other rooms, but two hallways jut out from either side of the bookshelf.

Five: To the right of the bookshelf is another larger shelf that reaches to the ceiling. Some people avoid using similar locations in the same rooms, but these are distinct looking, and I see them clearly. They work for me.

Six: A windowsill, large enough for my children to crawl into, is next to the large bookcase. The front yard is just beyond it.

Seven: A picture of a young boy, sitting on a pier, is on the wall. Actually, it's not there anymore. The picture was from years ago, when I first saw the house as a child. I thought it was a photograph of me. The picture's in another room now, but in my Mind Palace, it's on the wall.

Eight: Below the picture is a table with our television on in.

Nine: Underneath the table, is where we keep the Wii, DVDs (since I've never invested in a Blu-ray Player. Pfft. And I call myself a geek,) and sometimes, shoes that aren't supposed to go there.

Ten: To the right of that is the shoe-rack where the shoes ACTUALLY belong. If I can get my youngest child to remember that, we won't have to keep looking for shoes all the time. (If you're reading this, put your shoes where they go, sweetie.)

There. That's my first Mind Palace. It's small, so we can call it a Head-Hut. Do you have yours? No? Go ahead and make it. I'll wait.

All set? Congratulations. This is your first Memory Palace. Let's take a stroll through the place. Remember to use your own path, through the locations you've indicated yourself.

Enter the room in your mind. Take the images I'm about to describe, and imagine them at each location. We're going to make them a tad ludicrous. That's the point. Have them interact with the locations as much as possible.

One of the best tips I've come across for this type of visualization is to form crazy images. Make them funny. Better yet, make them shocking and obscene. This really works. However, if this book ever gets made into a movie, I'd like my children to be able to watch it. So we're going to steer away from the more obscene images. I'm shooting for something no worse than a hard PG.

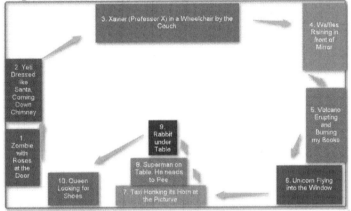

Location 1: A zombie appears, holding a dozen roses. Instead of "brain," he's moaning, "Lorraine..." I think he may have forgotten his zombie anniversary. (I'll say it again. Don't just read this. Picture it, in as much detail as you can, at your first location.)

Location 2: Do you know what a yeti is? It's those abominable snow monsters. I'm a big enough geek to know they're called yeti. The yeti I'm picturing is the one from the classic *Rudolph the Red Nosed Reindeer* stop-motion cartoon. Feel free to use whatever yeti image you can see the clearest. My second location is the fireplace, so the yeti is dressed like Santa Claus, coming out of the chimney. Make your yeti dressed up in a Santa outfit too.

Location 3: Xavier, otherwise known as Professor X, is sitting at location 3 in his wheelchair. This is Xavier as portrayed by Patrick Stewart in the first X-Men trilogy. His smooth shiny head is easy to visualize. In my image, I can see the brain waves flowing out of his skull.

Location 4: We've had enough pop culture for the moment. So, we're going to picture waffles. Mmmm. Waffles. The image has to be ludicrous to make it easier to remember, so we're going to have the waffles falling from the ceiling like rain. They're sticky with syrup, and it's going to get messy. Ugh. I just stepped in one, and now my foot's all sticky.

Location 5: Hopefully your 5th location cleans easily. You're going to put an erupting volcano there. Mine is the bookshelf, and the lava is going over all my books. They're burning, and it makes me sad.

(By the way, we're halfway through this exercise. You should be able to close your eyes, move through your new Memory Palace, and see a zombie with flowers, a yeti in a Santa suit, Xavier sitting with mind waves coming of his bald head, waffles raining from the ceiling, and a volcano. Make sure you see something before proceeding.)

Location 6: Did you know unicorns can fly? The one we're picturing can. It's flying around the 6th location, and ramming its horn into whatever is there. It makes a metallic ringing sound whenever it strikes.

Location 7: A Taxi is honking its horn. The driver is smoking a cigar, with his head out of the window, complaining that he's not leaving until you pay the fare. He's going to be disappointed too, because you're moving to the next location now.

Location 8: We're back to the pop culture references. Superman is here, right inside your Mind Palace. Bad news though, he's the one from the Zack Synder films, as portrayed by Henry Cavill. That means he's scowling a lot, wears a grayed out costume, and is one superhero brawl away from snapping somebody's neck. Since we have to make this memorable (unlike the Synder films,) he's also crossing his legs and dancing that *I-have-to-pee-but-don't-know-where-the-bathroom-is* dance. I secretly hope some of you are using a bathroom for your Memory Palace, because that would make this image even better.

Location 9: Almost there. Two more things to picture. First up, a ginormous rabbit is taking up all of location 9. It has glowing pink eyes, and because I know all rabbits are vicious killers, blood is dripping from its mouth. For some reason, it's also singing the Andrew Sisters song, *"Hello my baby, hello my honey, hello my ragtime gal."*

Location 10: A Queen, wearing a beautiful dress, and a gaudy crown, is at the last location. Since my location is a shoe rack, the queen in my mind is going through the shoes looking for something in glass.

Got it? Take your time. Really look around in your mind's eye, seeing the zombie, followed by the yeti. Actually marvel at how the light reflects off of Xavier's head, and maybe even chuckle at the thought of headlights. Smell the waffles raining from the ceiling. Feel your skin crackle from the heat as you get too close to the volcano, scold the unicorn for making too much noise, and decide whether or not you're going to pay for that imaginary taxi. When you get to the next spot, tell Zack Snyder's Superman it wouldn't kill him to smile every once in a while. Seriously. Be careful of the giant rabbit with the murderous eyes. And don't forget to properly greet the queen.

Now let's switch gears. We could have taken this a bit further, but this is more than sufficient to make the point. By show of hands, how many of you can say the alphabet backwards?

Probably a lot of us, right? Even if it's slower than it seems we should be able to? I generally have to sing the song in my head, then backtrack. It's hardest at the end, or rather the beginning. However, if you really took part in this little exercise, I bet you can fly through the first 10 letters of the backwards alphabet.

How?

Maybe you've already figured it out. I can tell how smart you are, since you've already bought this book.

Go through the journey we just made. Starting with Zombie, say out loud the first letter of each of the images we made.

Zombie, Yeti, Xavier, Waffles, Volcano, Unicorn, Taxi, Superman, Rabbit, Queen.

Z, Y, X, W, V, U, T, S, R, Q.

I know, right?

And if you really tried this, and it failed for some reason, try to figure out why. Is your image vivid enough? Is your path logical, without backtracking on itself? If not, try again, making sure of those two items. Now that you know what I'm up to, feel free to replace any of my images with one of your own. (For instance, replace the Henry Cavill Superman with the Christopher Reeve Superman. No one would blame you.)

If you want to complete the backwards alphabet, add the additional locations, and images to go along with them. We won't spend more time on that here, but I will give some starter ideas. You'll likely find that the images you come up with stick in the mind better than the ones someone else provide.

Starting with P: Popeye, Octopus, Nurse, Mouse, Lasagna, Kiefer Sutherland, Jellyfish, Ink spot, Hulk, Grass, Fireworks, Eggnog, Deadpool, Clown, Bryan Cranston, Armpit Noises.

Whether you use this Palace for the backwards alphabet, hopefully you've just realized something. You've realized that with a small amount of effort, anyone can have a stunning memory. It's how we're wired.

Welcome to a better world. A world where you don't have to write down shopping lists. A world where you can commit to memory pretty much anything you'd like. Some people use these techniques to memorize poetry or phone numbers, others the content of books and the names of people they met five years ago. I know of a book by Anthony Meivier dedicated to memorizing the vocabulary of other languages, with reviews of people who used these techniques to become fluent in those languages.

What was it Morpheus said? "You take the red pill, you stay in Wonderland, and I show you how deep the rabbit hole goes." And that's just it. There's no telling how deep this can get. The ground's not even the beginning of the limit.

Hmm. That sounded better in my head. Let's just move on. It's time I introduced myself.

2. How It Started (Or, Why I Hate My Boss)

My name is Scott. I'm an addict. I can hear you now. "Hello, Scott." Hello yourselves, and thanks for your support.

But you know what? Let's be fair to people with real addictions. Maybe it's wrong to call myself an addict. I don't drink. I don't smoke. Aside from allergy medicine and the occasional Advil, I stay away from drugs. I'll call a spade a spade (though later in this book I'll call it a candle, a swan, and other non-spade things.)

I have an addictive personality. It's why I can juggle, why I'm not allowed to gamble, why I've seen every episode of the New Doctor Who Series (hereafter referred to as NuWho,) and why I hate my boss.

This is all his fault.

I remember it like it was yesterday. After all, this is a book about memorization.

See, I work for a great company. (I really believe that, so Boss, if you're reading this, please don't take this chapter the wrong way.) My company cares about its employees, and it shows it in numerous ways, including a new break room. Boy, was that nice. They put in hardwood floors, cable television, lounge sofas, and games on the lunch table. One of the games? A Rubik's cube.

Once the room was ready, they served sushi and hibachi at our *grand-opening-of-the-break-room-party*. And then two horrible thing happened.

Niall solved the cube.

In case you're counting, that's both of the horrible things. Niall impressed everyone by solving the cube. Not me. I couldn't do it. Not only that, I was bested by a guy that doesn't even know how to spell his own name. (Niall, if you're reading this, it's N-E-I-L.)

Naturally, I went home and taught myself how to solve the cube. Who wouldn't? (As it turns out, nobody else in the world. Or at least nobody else in the company. That's who.)

Don't worry. You haven't accidentally bought the wrong book. This isn't a cube solving book, so there's no need to go over those pesky algorithms like R, U, R', F', R, U, R', U', R', F, R2, U', R'. Suffice to say, over the course of that weekend, I managed to get my average solving time down to a stunning three minute average.

I came back to work, armed with my shiny new cube, proud to show off my newfound ability.

Nobody cared. That should only come as a surprise to people without my capacity for obsessing over bright, shiny things.

"That's fine," I said to myself. "I didn't do this for the attention. I did it for the fun of learning a new skill. Hmm. Maybe if I get faster, it'll impress somebody."

So, I spent a few more days learning something called the Roux method, and got my average closer to a minute.

Still nobody cared, except for my wife. Well, *concerned* is the more accurate word. She was mostly concerned about my mounting cube collection.

Me? I was just glad I managed to get sucked into cubing AFTER getting married. It meant I didn't have to worry about my geekiness keeping me from ever meeting a girl.

Fast forward even further. I'd given up cubing... as a means to impress people. I can never give it up completely. Who knows when I'll randomly find myself in front of a cube? It happened the other evening, at a restaurant. Some little girl had one out on the table. Fortunately, I (just barely) managed to restrain myself from offering to solve it for her. When she finally picked it up, she solved it quicker than I ever have.

I keep at it. It's fun for a few minutes on airplanes. And, when I was learning the Roux method, I could close my eyes at night and practically see myself solving the cube. Why, I bet I could even learn how to solve it blindfolded.

Guess where this is going.

Like so many fly-by-night hobbies before cubing, my addiction morphed on the spot into memorization. You can't solve a cube blindfolded without first memorizing the position of every single piece.

No worries. This book will in fact *not* teach you how to solve a cube, blindfolded or otherwise. If you're interested, it will share some techniques that will aid in the memorization needed to do both tasks.

I read and researched, practiced the techniques, and repeated. Several times. Through that, I've come to more than a few conclusions, many of which I'll share throughout the course of this book. One of them is that most speedcubers are horrible at teaching their methods. You can't just say, "It's intuitive," and expect that to help somebody.

However, the most amazing conclusion is this. An average memory can be a *so-outstanding-my-mouth-fell-open-in-awe* memory, if used the right way. Your memory, harnessed correctly, is enough to astound your friends, even if you never solve a Rubik's cube faster than that know it all girl at the pizza restaurant.

Even memory champions like Ed Cooke, claim not to possess amazing memories. They've simply learned how to use what they already possessed. It's the same thing we all have.

My memory? I'm not going to lie. Prior to this journey, I thought it was pretty good. Mainly because I could memorize huge chunks of dialog during my acting days. I even, briefly, learned long passages of Scripture, up to three chapters at a time, to perform dramatically in churches.

Here's the rub. The way I memorized things was the same reason so many people think they can't do it at all. I didn't possess amazing memory. I just had hyper focus, getting drawn into the things that captured my attention. I didn't mind spending hours a day learning something, only to forget it a few days after I'd finished with it.

That's the thing though. I forgot it all. Quickly. If I needed to perform any of it again, I either had to rehearse every day, or do some crash-course style studying a couple of days before. That's not memorization.

Read my lips. No, scratch that. This isn't a video blog. Read my words instead. There. Is. A. Better. Way.

A week ago, I showed a friend the most recent deck of cards I'd memorized. Because I haven't purposefully cleared out the order of those cards, I can still do it right now. The other, less trivial things I've memorized such as people's names, and geography facts I'd always wanted to know, are there for good. Because I've found the better path.

Back before learning this, memorizing those tons of lines I mentioned wasn't easy, but at least I knew the worst possible way of doing it.

Rote.

Rote memory.

Rote memory is.

Rote memory is the.

Rote memory is the worst.

Rote memory is the worst way.

Rote memory is the worst way to.

Rote memory is the worst way to memorize.

Rote memory is the worst way to memorize anything.

One Example. For a church production, I memorized the Sermon on the Mount. It's three chapters long, roughly 2500 words. I should have used a Memory Palace, and put things in it like a poor ghost with her empty pockets hanging out, standing in front of pearly gates. That would have triggered the phrase, "Blessed are the poor in spirit, for theirs is the kingdom of heaven."

Instead, I learned a chapter a day, in the exact same way I typed that thing about rote memory.

Like this:

Blessed are the poor.

Blessed are the poor in spirit.

Blessed are the poor in spirit, for theirs.

Blessed are the poor in spirit, for theirs is the kingdom of heaven.

For three straight chapters.

Imagine, spending hours a day learning it that way. No need for me to imagine it. I did exactly that, four or five times. Like I said before, every time I was asked to perform again, I had to start over. Sure, it was easier the next time around, because I remembered large portions of it. But I never LEARNED it. So I always had to relearn it. Worse still, I taught other people to memorize things this way.

I should give them all free copies of this book. If I could remember them all, I would, but this was long before I learned how to remember names.

Now knowing it without losing the information is simple. How?

By employing techniques like the one we started with. Hopefully you participated in the exercise, because it showed how you can do this. And it doesn't involve mindless repetition. These methods are better than rote repetition in the same way that a relaxing day at the beach is better than getting stabbed with a rusty knife.

It's going to be fun. Get ready for an added bonus if you're a geek like me, because this provides an opportunity to talk a bit about Doctor Who and Star Wars.

In a few pages you'll learn how to memorize numbers. How to remember shopping lists. Names and faces. Addresses. Poetry. And, yes (finally!) how to impress somebody with your memory.

You're going to learn how to memorize a deck of 52 cards. Or even multiple decks, for that matter.

But first, I have to tell you about some dead guy.

3. Location, Location, Location

The reason we have the memory method I'll spend most of the book covering, is because a few centuries ago, a tragedy occurred at a Roman feast. The roof collapsed, killing everybody left in the room. When the dust cleared, only a poet had survived. I'm not saying that's the tragedy. I've never even read any of his poems.

Put another way, way back in the 5th Century, Simonides of Ceos was the life of the party. When he left it, the room went dead.

What? Too soon?

Here's the full story. The banquet hall's roof collapsed, right as Simonides left the room. And, despite my flippant tone, nothing about the grizzly scene was humorous. Rescuers dug through the debris, first looking for survivors, then for remains.

Only Simonides lived, and that's only because he had left the room to meet some people outside. Nobody even knew for sure who had died.

Nobody except Simonides. He realized that, just by looking into his mind's eye, he knew where the table was. He *saw* the host. The people seated next to the host. On down the line, through each of the tables, he vividly recalled where everyone was, just as he had crossed the threshold of the door.

Fortunately for the deceased families, Simonides was able to identify the lost. Because of the technique, he's credited as being the discoverer. Kind of like when Newton discovered gravity. Before the apple hit Newton on the head, people weren't constantly surprised that things fell down instead of up. Newton quantified it for people.

And Simonides was able to recognize the power of location as it applies to remembering things. Things like grocery lists, important dates, every Doctor to travel in the Tardis, the poetry he wrote, and even the names of your former banquet companions.

It's called the Method of Loci. Loci is a Latin word meaning *places*. That's why you'll see what I'm describing here as the Loci Method, Memory Palaces, or Roman Rooms. The last name for this is because it originated in Rome.

Here's why the Memory Palace works.

You can remember places that you're familiar with.

And believe it or not, this is mostly true. I know someone, let's call her Nancy. Nancy could never find her way to her sister's house, even though she'd been there dozens of times. Every time she visited, Nancy's sister — let's call her Susanna — could always expect a call asking her where Nancy got lost.

Then, along came GPS, and things actually got worse. I'm still not clear on why, but the combination of Nancy's bad directional memory and the GPS guidance ended up with her getting lost even quicker.

I'd love to tell you that prior to writing this book, I worked with Nancy, and now she's a memory champion with the ability to memorize road names and directions. I might get away with it too. Throw in a quote from Nancy saying, "I've never learned anything that's changed my life more dramatically than this, Scott. A million thanks for literally showing me the way." Alas, such is my integrity that I would never dream of doing such a thing here. Plus, there's a good chance that word would get back to either Nancy or Susanna, so I'd better not.

Nancy got lost on the way to Susanna's, but even she never got lost in her own house. Given that, I bet even she could use location for memory improvement.

The places people are most familiar with are gateways to memory. They can practically see them. The brain remembers in images. That's why so many people can remember faces but not names. Count me formerly among people like that. (It's almost a shame. I loved to joke that, "I'm terrible with names, but I'm horrible with faces." Alas, I can't do that anymore.) You see the face. Not the other way around.

Because we're visual, we can picture putting things in those places, and those images stick. If you went through my introductory exercise, can you still see the locations along the way? Can you still see the zombie? The taxi? Superman trying not to pee in the middle of the room?

I can, and for years I've argued that I wasn't a visual learner.

A common theme in memory books is that anybody can perform these amazing feats of memory. Are you not a visual person? Not a visual learner?

Doesn't matter. I've never been a visual person either. So why would I advocate the visual techniques forthcoming in this book? Because Amazon pays me a percentage of every book sold, that's why.

There's a better reason, and I fully acknowledge that it's circular reasoning. But sometimes, circular reasoning works, and I can prove it. Do a google search for "things you can't find on google." You can use this link: http://bit.ly/1rX7W7w

I just did it, and got 489,000,000 results. Go figure.

It doesn't matter if you're not a visual person, because sing these visual methods skills trains you to be able to use the visual methods needed.

Yeah, I know. It's best not to think too hard about that. Just like it's maybe best not to think about how the method came about in the first place.

I've always felt slow when it came to conjuring images in my head.

If you go to my house, you'll see a bookshelf in the right corner of the living room that reaches from the floor to the ceiling. It's crammed with books. To the left of the hallway door is another bookshelf that sits at just below waist height. It's also overflowing with books. So is another bookshelf in my bedroom. And that's not all my books. They're scattered throughout the house. I've read them all. (That's Hyperbole. I've probably only read 98% of them.)

You know how a good fiction story plays like a movie in your mind? They almost never did for me, until I started using these forthcoming visual memory techniques. Some people hate seeing a movie based on a book before reading the book. They want the luxury of seeing the pictures their minds come up with first.

Me? It didn't bother me either way. Look, I've read all five books in *The Hitchhiker's Guide to the Galaxy* a dozen times. Easily. And to this day I have no idea what Zaphod Beeblebrox looks like. Bad example. I've seen the film once, and I still don't know. I just know it's not like what the film said.

Better example. Until I saw the *Lord of the Rings* trilogy, I had no picture in my head at all of many of the characters. Didn't need to. My mind deals well with concepts, and I had the concept of Frodo just fine. Until seeing it on film, I had no idea what Frodo looked like, or that Samwise Gamgee looked like a Notre Dame walk-on.

Naturally, I wondered if I had the aptitude for visual memory techniques like Loci. Could I really make a Mind Palace like Sherlock did on that BBC show? Stranger things have happened, like me actually watching a BBC show. Still, I've seen my imagination, and it's never had special effects like Sherlock's did.

I made that exact point to my brother-in-law, Kris, convinced that most people's minds worked the same way. Kris, who has always been great at memorization, said that his images are exactly like that. Good. That means it's all the more likely he can still visualize the final score, when I put up 100 points against him in Madden Football. (Hi Kris. I hope you're reading this.) Whether your visualization special effects are as poor as mine, or as great as my brother-in-law's, you've got more than enough imagination to make this work.

We're hard wired to remember this way. I can see the rooms in my Palaces, along with the crazy images I've created for them. They get wilder the more I practice, which makes them more vivid than ever. That makes them easier to remember.

And all those books I keep reading? They've never been clearer in my mind than now. Frankly, I'm considering rereading several novels again. Maybe I'll even start with the Hitchhiker's Guide again. My imagination feels like it's finally free, after years of being locked up. (That's a scary thought for anyone who's known me for any length of time.)

I wanted you to know this. Now let's build more Palaces together.

4. Your Body Is A Palace

We've already built a small Memory Palace. What's next?
Realizing that just about anything can be a Palace.

I first learned about this technique as it related to
cubing. A Rubik's-like cube contains 20 pieces. Four edge
pieces, on three different layers make up the first twelve, then
eight corner pieces round out the 20.

I rejected most of the common methods for memorizing
the positions as being needlessly complicated. That's when I
stumbled upon loci, or Memory Palaces. Oddly enough, I
found the cube based explanations on several websites to be
needlessly simple.

They taught me to build a Palace with enough rooms,
using only four locations in each room, hopefully around the
corners.

Five rooms with four corners? That seemed hard at
first, but I figured it out within minutes.

A mnemonic device is any technique used to help
remember and recall information. This includes rhymes,
songs, alliteration, and visual cues. Think of mnemonics as a
shortcut to memory.

I'd already created my own mnemonics for each
combination of the colors. I then memorized a scrambled
cube, making only two mistakes. Reviewing the cube helped
me do it again with no mistakes.

Sure, my chest puffed out. I was thrilled. Amazed.

And, maybe, just a little bit disappointed.

Based on the cubing explanation, I thought a Memory Palace had to be a house. It had to have no more than 4 locations per room.

That seemed so limiting. I could clearly see other locations in the rooms. For that matter, the first Palace I built had six rooms unused. Surely, there had to be even greater possibilities, and better ways to create the Palaces.

Turns out, there were.

A Palace can be created out of any location. It doesn't even have to be an enclosed structure.

Streets, nature trails, vehicles, and more can be used. If it can be visualized, it works for storing information.

I know of people who use video games to store things. I still know the location of almost every dungeon in the original Legend of Zelda. I'm a bit iffy on the 3rd and 5th dungeons, but I bet I could find them within minutes if I had access to the game. In fact, just thinking about them brings back the theme song. Looks like I'll be humming it to myself for the rest of the night. Great.

If it helps, stop calling these receptacles of memory, *Palaces*. For instance, if I ever decide to encode information in Zelda's land of Hyrule, you can bet I'll refer to that as my *Memory Dungeon*.

The point? Make Palaces out of any location or area you know like the back of your hand.

Speaking of which—

That first Palace I mentioned above? It's my house. When I used it for cubes, I strolled through the living room, into the main bedroom, the larger bathroom, the kitchen, and finally down the basement. That left out two bedrooms, a bath, two hallways, the attic, and in fact many areas of the basement.

What a waste. That's part of what led me to researching loci, and ultimately, to writing this book. Well, that and my boss for buying the Rubik's cube in the first place.

Thanks again, Boss.

I decided to use that first Palace for more permanent information. I'd always felt like I should know the capital of every state. Now I do. They're stored in my carport, the living room, two bathrooms, two bedrooms, and the hallway.

In the meantime, I needed a more temporary place to use for solving cubes. By this point, I'd already created a huge Palace for temporarily memorizing decks of cards, but I didn't want to use the same one for this.

Then I stumbled across the idea of using the body as a location. If memory serves, and it does, I first read about this in a book by a memory champion named Dominic O'Brien. I'll say more about that book, and others, in the resource section of this book.

Back to the body as location. Just think about it. Have you ever forgotten where your chin was? How about the left knee? I doubt it.

Instead of notepads, or smart phones, I started using my own body to store temporary lists.

I needed to pick up milk, orange juice, bottled water, and coffee from the store. No problem. In my vision, my right foot started sweating milk. It actually gushed out of my shoe, leaving a milky white trail everywhere I stepped. My left foot was no better. It turned into a carton of orange juice. That made it hard to walk, because if I set my foot down too hard, the cartoon might break, mixing the juice and milk. And if they mix, they turn sour.

By the way, when using this technique, always start with the right side. That way, you'll know you have another side left.

Anyway, I next moved to my right knee, which had a spigot of water protruding from it. That's right. I had water on the knee.

My left knee must have been busted, because I heard it grinding when I walked. Coffee shook loose with each step. I even smelled the grounds.

See? Milk, orange juice, water, and coffee. And I didn't even have to waist anything.

What did I do once I made this list? I sloshed.

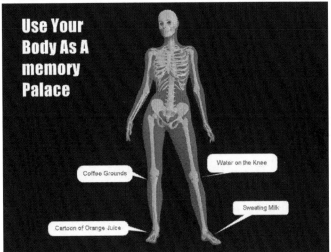

Original Image by Bernhard Ungerer. Modified and used under a Creative Commons Attribution 4.0 International License.
https://www.flickr.com/photos/bernhard_ungerer/2598558747/

Now, I use my body for any transient information I have to remember, including the cube's colors. For those twenty locations, I use both pairs of feet, shins, knees, thighs, hands, elbows, shoulders, eyes, and ears. After that, I use my mouth, and top it all off with my head.

Be creative as you create your Memory Palaces. Make as many as you can.

I tend to figure out how many locations I'll need, and create the mnemonics first, then figure out the best Palace location for each. Once you've exhausted your childhood home, current location, schools, work places, and family's houses, branch out to other types of locations.

It's a great way to get to know yourself.

Now, make a ten item list, memorize it, and go to the store. You're only allowed to buy what you remember. See how many items you come back with correctly. If it works for all ten items, fantastic! If not, congratulations. You just saved some money. Just remember to focus on the images the next time you make a shopping list.

5. It's Not A Story

Let's pause for a moment and talk about this whole Memory Palace thing.

The images built along the path should be riveting. They should be hard to look away from. They're so interesting, the mind can't help but remember them. It's almost like watching a story.

Almost.

I've spent my life learning stories. Reading them. Writing them. Which reminds me, don't forget to check out *Already Seen* from the Amazon store. I highly recommend it.

What we create on these journeys through our Palaces may seem like stories, but they're not. If they are, they're probably terrible ones.

Early on, I made the mistake of trying to turn these images into a story. Each method gets easier with time. Starting out though, it seemed impossible. Why? Because some places referred to them as making up stories. Coming up with the right images can seem challenging enough without turning it all into some kind of coherent plot.

One of my first Palaces included images with a wrestler, a giant tree, a cheerleader, Santa Claus, and a blue devil. I probably could have turned all of those into some kind of story, along with all the other images to come, but I had to make the story move from location to location.

The wrestler sprang from the couch cushions, onto the giant tree growing violently from my attic door. He was trying to get to the cheerleader (Save the cheerleader, save the world,) but she jumped just as he reached her. Fortunately, Santa Claus swooped down from the bookcase, and caught her. But the wicked blue devil in the windowsill threw its basketball of evil (GO HEELS!) and hit the sleigh.

As effective as using locations are for storing memories, getting somebody to buy into the method can be a hard sale. If I'd tried to convince you that you had to build a story like that, you'd have stopped reading by now. And good for you, because that would have been the proper response.

Lots of otherwise good resources refer to these journeys through remembered locations as stories. It feels like making a story. Sometimes, locations in my Palaces interact with each other. Emperor Palpatine has hurled force lightning from his location in the education games at Barnes and Noble, frying poor R2D2 in the religion section. But then, I reached the information kiosk, covered in bacon and eggs. That's not a story. That's a mess.

If you've been thinking that these Memory Palaces work like that, relax. Sometimes an image is just an image. That doesn't make it a story.

I'm glad I got that off my chest. Let's move on.

6. I Don't Even See The Cards Anymore

The first day I learned to shuffle a deck and memorize it, I showed several people.

"Can you show me a magic trick?" I asked.

"Er—"

"No, it's easy. Here, cut this deck, and place the cut half face up."

After they did this, I said something like, "Ah. The 3 of Clubs. Good. Go ahead and turn the Queen of Diamonds over. Good. Follow that by the— Jack of Spades. Fantastic! I bet you can do the 8 of Spades now. The 9 of Hearts. One more. Turn over the Ace of Spades. That's amazing! How did you do that?"

Somehow, cutting to the middle of the deck and reading out 8-12 cards in a row impressed them more doing all 52 would have.

I impressed a lot of people that day. (Finally.)

How did I do it? It's kind of funny. Not, "ha-ha funny." But it's still amusing.

I spent an entire weekend learning to solve the Rubik's cube. I followed that up with more hours and days than I'd care to admit, if I even remembered, trying to get faster.

So far I've impressed exactly two people with that ability. By that time, I'd been working on it for over two months.

It happened on a plane. I had the dreaded middle seat, parked between two women. I pulled the cube out, like one does. The lady on my left asked if she could scramble it for me. Then she timed me. This was back before I learned a more advanced method, so I told her I'd solve it in under two minutes. When I did, she said, "Nice." The one on my right said, "Wow."

For the rest of the four hour plane ride, we didn't say another word to each other. And I'd solved it so fast, I didn't even get my full fifteen minutes of fame.

Contrast that to the card trick. I spent less than a day learning to memorize cards. Granted, I'd already put in some time learning about how to build a Mind Palace. By then, I'd created several rooms and used them to memorize the colors on my Rubik's cube.

All I needed was to come up with 52 locations, and a few images. (There are ways to lower this number considerably. We'll get to that in a couple of chapters.)

I took a walk around my future Memory Palace for cards, took some pictures on my phone for reference, and spent a few fun minutes charting a path. I didn't even really have to memorize it — just make sure I knew the right path.

And I needed to come up with mnemonic devices for each of the cards. That was even more fun.

Remember that a mnemonic device is any technique used to help remember and recall information. We've already seen this. When you remembered Volcano for the letter V, that was a device.

When I remembered handcuffs for the number 3, it was the same thing.

Sounds like a lot of work, right?

Maybe. But it's fun, and not nearly as time consuming as it sounds. Plus, the payoff is enormous. I'm showing how to do this for cards, but the same techniques can be used for just about anything.

I didn't time myself, but I figured all of this throughout the course of a single day. That took place in brief spurts. I wrote everything down for reference, then memorized my first deck of cards on the very first try.

Some of you might be wondering if it's worth the effort learning how to memorize a deck of cards.

Of course it is. I've already shown that it's easy to impress people with it. That's all my ego needs. My mnemonic device for the Ace of Hearts, (Hearts being things I love) is picturing myself. Psychoanalyze that if you must.

Here are two additional reasons why this is worthwhile.

First: This is a fantastic way to flex your memory muscles. You'll build an impressive Mind Palace, and grow intimately familiar with it.

Second: It makes you virtually unbeatable at Solitaire.

Here's the thing about learning how to memorize 52 cards. It's the same thing as all the other methods we'll discuss. Just like the alphabet images, you have to make this method something that will resonate with you. I've read through three other explanations about how to do this before developing my own variation.

Each technique had a reason for me rejecting them. The first method I read about involved heavy reliance on something called the Major System. I'll go over it in detail later in the book, and even revisit how to apply it to memorizing cards. Even though I've come to appreciate that system, early on it didn't appeal to me at all.

I've successfully used the Major System to memorize several random numbers. It's partly what I use for memorizing my airline travel itinerary these days. But, cards were one of the first things I learned, and at the time the Major System seemed hopelessly complex. It isn't. It just seemed that way.

So I'm sharing my initial method first. It was the best for me, starting out. I think it's the easiest way to begin, and a natural progression from building the more simplistic Memory Palace we created earlier. But again, make this your own. If some of my images work for you, by all means use them. Later in the book, I'll show a more advanced method that builds on what's shown here.

The prep work is the hardest part. Honestly. But, it's also kind of fun. And, it's amazing how quickly it can be done. I did an Amazon Search for similar books before writing this one. One title said something along the lines of, *Learn to Memorize Cards in 4 weeks.*"

Pfft. I scoffed. Really. I literally, actually scoffed. Didn't realize what a delightfully scornful sound scoffing can make until then. I know for a fact this can be accomplished in less than a day, with most of that time brainstorming about Doctor Who and Star Wars. And who wouldn't want to brainstorm about Doctor Who and Star Wars? (If the answer is yourself, feel free to keep reading. Just know I've lost some respect for you already.)

The first step is to assign an image to every card in the deck. This is the mnemonic device. Remember, the more crazy the image, the better. My image for the 8 of Spades is a snowman, because the 8 looks like a snowman. When I visualize this in my Memory Palace, I have the snowman doing all sorts of crazy things. The early ones melted. Then, they started pulling snow out of their bodies, and throwing snowballs at passersby. Sometimes it's a hoard of time snowmen, building a fort. The more crazy the image, the more likely I am to remember it.

Cards Image by Scott Hughey. Snowman Image by Tine Steiss and used under an Attribution –ShareAlike 2.0 License
https://www.flickr.com/photos/herrberta/

I'm not even going to tell you what my image for the 5 of Clubs, an anthropomorphic broccoli stalk, has done in my imagination. Not because the stalk was bad, but because it was just plain weird.

I recommend writing what each card's image will be in a memory journal. You won't have to reference it much after the first time or two, but it's helpful getting started. It also lets the mind relax, knowing there's a backup somewhere.

As you create images, try to come up with as many nouns as possible. It's easier to visualize a thing like a cow, or even a burning cow, than it is to picture a concept, like hunger.

The second step is to come up with a Memory Palace that will have 52 different locations. That sounds daunting, I know. It's the hardest part of this entire process. But, pick a place you're familiar with, and you'll be surprised by how quickly it adds up.

If you're too intimidated for 52 locations right now, go ahead and create a Palace of 13 locations, and follow along with one suit. Later, you can add more locations, or use one of the more advanced methods I'll discuss later that will lower the number of locations needed.

The last part is the best. Take a deck of cards. Shuffle them. Then turn them over and make your journey. Feel free to only shuffle one or two suites. Or only try memorizing 13 random cards selected from the entire deck. This gives you the confidence to do more and more.

Here's every image I use except for the Hearts. Those are of people and/or things I love, and they're deeply personal. Plus, I don't want to get anybody's feelings hurt because I didn't list them. (Sorry, Veronica. We both know this is the best way to spare everyone's feelings.)

I'll explain the reasoning behind these as best I can.

Let's start with the Diamonds. I chose Star Wars for Diamonds, because stars kind of look like Diamonds. And, it's Star Wars. How could I not? (That reminds me. Thank you J.J. Abrams, for making Star Wars awesome again. If you're reading this, please feel free to leave an endorsement. Or offer me a cameo in an upcoming film. I can memorize dialog in less than 12 parsecs.)

The Diamond suit goes as follows:

A: Death Star. It's the Empire's Ace in the hole. It's also the screenwriter's.

2: R2D2. For hopefully obvious reasons.

3: C3PO. See Above

4: Greedo. (He's the green alien that would have survived, except HAN! SHOT! FIRST! He only appears in Episode 4. Too bad Han didn't shoot first in Episode 7 too. He might have survived. Er... Spoiler Alert. Sorry.

5: The Wampa. For those of you not geeky enough, this is the snow monster on Hoth from Episode 5. Luke cut its arm off. Guess that means he got was coming to him by the end of the film. Er, spoiler alert.

6: Ewoks. From Episode 6.

7: Finn. This number had me stumped. I mean, several characters appeared first in Episode 7, but which one to use? Then, I realize that Finn sounds like seven. Se-Finn. PLUS, his designation is FN plus the cell number Leia was held in on the first Death Star. FN-2187. Ends in Seven. Genius. Sometimes, in my Memory Palace, Finn appears as himself. Sometimes he's got the Stormtrooper helmet with the bloody palm print on it. And sometimes, there's another Stormtrooper yelling, "Traitor!" at Finn before attacking him. That character would have made a great image, except I already had—

8: BB-8. And if you don't know why this fits, you've not been paying attention.

9: This stumped me too. Maybe I'm missing something, but nothing is obvious. I assume Supreme Leader Snoke is going to be the big bad in Episode 9, so he's the image I use. (I'm calling it here everyone... Snoke is Darth Plagueis. Google it if you want to know why. Or, you can buy the sound tracks to Episodes 3 and 7, and figure it out on your own. Maybe I can get Disney to pay for that unintentional product placement too.) Since Andy Serkis played Snoke, I sometimes have fun and substitute Gollum instead. Oddly enough, I've never once substituted Richard Kneeland into my Memory Palace. That's Jennifer Garner's boss from 13 Going On 30, played by... Andy Serkis.

10: Slave Princess Leia. Not that *I'm* saying she was a perfect 10 in Jedi, but some people do. The image fits. I've tried putting Rey here, because she's probably my favorite character from The Force Awakens. Even though her powers and abilities are either off the chart, or 10 out of 10, but the association never worked as well as I wanted it to.

J: Luke Skywalker.

Q: Queen Amidala.

K: Palpatine. He's the King, or rather the Emperor, of the Galaxy. At least he was a long time ago in a galaxy far, far away.

Hopefully these images will either be useful to you, or of great assistance in creating your own. Do you enjoy any other fandoms? Use them. Harry Potter would work just as well as Star Trek, or Marvel comics. Be advised that if you choose Twilight, you can't use Star Wars also. I mean, Stars fit diamonds for sure, but where else are you going to store the sparkling vampires?

What about Doctor Who? Guess how many Doctors there have been? If you include the War Doctor, 13, the exact same number of cards in a suit. That would have been easy, but I worried about having too many doctors, and the lines blurring. I only have 4 actual doctors in my 52 Card Memory Palace system. I wasn't going to indulge myself and share this list, but I'm lying. I was always going to indulge myself. It's the same reason I went to Amazon Prime when Netflix lost the series in the United States. (It only counts as product placement if they pay you for it. How about it Amazon? Interested in throwing a little extra my way? Hello? No? Ah, well. It was worth a try.)

A: The Sonic Screwdriver is the Doctor's/Screenwriter's Ace in the Hole.

2: Tardis. I kept trying to make this the Ace or the King in my mind, and it never worked. The *T* sound in both Tardis and Two works.

3: Amy Pond. Because she seemed to be involved in a love triangle.

4: A colorful scarf, just like the 4th Doctor wore.

5: Broccoli. Like the 5th Doctor wore. To all you non-whovians, I am not making this up. Also, if you're a non-whovian, find a way to watch the *Blink* episode. It has nothing to do with the number 5, but you'll still thank me.

6: Clara. This works for me, and I'm not certain why. If you count the major companions and include Rory, then sure, she's the 6th NuWho companion. I'll go with that as a reason.

7: Cybermen. Cyber starts out sounding like seven.

8: Daleks. Daleks kind of look like the number 8. Also, Daleks were the 8th enemy the First Doctor faced. Also, I just made that last part up.

9: Christopher Eccleston. The Ninth Doctor. We're not counting the War Doctor as part of the numbering scheme. Here's how you count to 10 in the Doctor Who Universe. 1, 2, 3, 4, 5, 6, 7, 8, War, 9, 10.

10: David Tennant. My Doctor.

J: I could have gone with the immortal Jack, but then where would I have put this next image? Jack is the Eleventh Card. Matt Smith was the eleventh doctor. If I hadn't already found David, Matt would have been my Doctor. Sometimes I picture a bow tie instead, because Bow Ties are cool.

Q: River Song is, of course, the Queen of Doctor Who. Another side note. A friend of mine named his child River, after River Song. Even though I sometimes suspect he did it so that when the kid races through the house and his wife asks what all the noise in the living room is, Andy can say, "A River Runs Through It."

K: Peter Capaldi. The twelfth Doctor. Of course, I can also get away just visualizing his eyebrows.

I initially tried using NuWho's major companions as the first few choices, but that didn't work either. Sure, you can go Rose, Martha, Donna, Amy, Clara, and maybe even Bill. But then what? And that's not to mention how Donna appeared before Martha, but not as a companion, and so did Clara. (So did Amy, but she wasn't Amy yet. Come to think of it, so did Martha.) And it just gets worse if you add in the others. Does Mickey count? Does Rory? Sure, but then what about Jack? Or Wilfred? Absolutely not! Great man, sure, but I'll never forgive him for being the end of the 10th Doctor.

The only reason he entered that glass chamber was to give the Doctor something to die for later on. And Wilfred, the Doctor already told you that someone would knock four times, heralding the Doctor's demise. You knew! Why not knock three times? Five? No wonder he got so mad. I could have used you for the number four, but I would never give you that honor.

Ah. Wow. It feels good to get that off my chest. Back to the cards.

Notice that I substituted images where possible. Seeing huge, bushy eyebrows springing up from the ground like a net trap, and suspending people in the air is a memorable picture, so it works. When I do use the characters as images, I try to give them dialog. "I'm sorry. I'm so, so sorry.

I'm not including the Hearts, but you may benefit from hearing my initial version of the Spades. I'll discuss later how I've since modified this list.

To me, spades are just things. So, I have a list of things. Early on, when I was fighting the Major Memory System, I mostly borrowed a single digit numbering system for single digits. This system uses images that resemble numbers in some form or another. That's what I started using for Spades:

0: No card for zero. But, before I learned the forthcoming numbering system, I used an egg or a basketball for 0.

A: Candle. Because the A is the #1 card, and a candle is a straight line like a 1.

2: Swan. The number is sort of shaped like a swan.

3: Handcuffs. Some people also use butterflies, but that never worked for me.

4: A Sailboat. The number is shaped like the sail. Often, this becomes Styx singing, "Come sail away..." I started using a flag here like some people use for 4, but had a hard time making that into memorable images.

5: Looks like a sea horse. So I'll picture that, or more often a real horse. Sometimes it's also a snake.

6: Cherries. I still need a better image though. Maybe I'll start using sewage, now that I'm better at the Major system.

7: This is an axe, or a boomerang. If I visualize a boomerang, it's usually a batarang like Batman uses.

8: Usually I make this a Snowman, because they make for great images. I'll also use an ice skater making a figure eight. I tried imagining infinity for this but there was just no end to the possibilities.

9: A balloon. And that's the one I struggle with most, possibly because I dislike balloons. Clowns? No issues. Balloons? Ugh. Again, now that I'm using the Major system for other things, I could start imagining "Poo." Not to get off track, but I suddenly feel the need to clarify- the Major System doesn't necessarily stick to things you'd find in a sewer.

10: This looks like a fork and a dinner plate. I imagine dinner.

J: The eleventh card. This becomes lightsabers fighting each other. When I added the Star Wars theme for diamonds, I thought that might keep me from remembering the suits, so I changed it to swords, and promptly forgot the image each time I came to it. I switched back to the special effects version with no difficulty in calling a spade, a spade. (Can I make that same joke twice? Guess so, cause I just did.)

Q: Roses. A dozen roses for the Queen.

K: Baker's Dozen. I picture bread, usually along with the smell of it baking.

That's an interesting phenomenon in itself. I haven't read much about smell as it applies to loci, but when I have an object with a distinct smell like roses or bread, I'll sniff when I come to the number. Often, I don't even remember it's something to smell until I sniff. And I always remember. It is well documented that smells are tied to memory. This, to me, is further evidence.

I try to incorporate some form of all the senses. Sight and smell are obvious. I haven't spent much time tasting my objects, but I have felt the stickiness of the dinner plate, and listened to my characters saying their lines. It all helps.

There you have the images for cards. Take some time to create some for yourself. Write them down. Don't store them in the Memory Palace just yet. That comes later, when you've shuffled the deck.

Once you have the images set, it's time to create a Palace to hold all your cards.

I took my daughter to Barnes and Noble the day I was working on this. My face lifted into a smile big enough to make the security guard notice me, and pay special attention to the guy with the crazed look on his face. That always happens when I enter big book stores. But this time, it was because I saw loci everywhere!

I *knew* this store. Moreover, I wanted to use the houses I'd lived in over the years for more permanent storage space. Book stores constantly change their inventory. How perfect could that be?

In anticipation of a question I had starting out, yes. It's okay to reuse Palaces for short term memory items like this. Some people wait an hour, or a day, to let the memory clear out. I imagine throwing gasoline on the place, burning everything in it. 451 degrees Fahrenheit — the temperature at which Memory Palaces catch fire.

Until I wrote those last two sentences, it didn't occur to me how troubling destroying the Palace in this manner might sound. Let's just assume that one of the Doctors manages to get everyone out alive, and save all the books too. It'd be easy too. The 2 of Clubs is bigger on the inside.

Back to the cards. Check to make sure you know your mnemonics. Check to make sure you know your path through your Memory Palace. Remember, the path you take should be logical. Don't cross the streams. Avoid backtracking over your path.

Some people also find it hampering to end the path with no exit. For that reason, if possible, have the path end at a door.

That door can lead to another Palace. Say, the one where you're remembering the order of initial appearances (by comic publication) of the major Marvel superheroes. Let's see, Fantastic Four, Ant-man, Hulk, Sub-Mariner (post Golden Age,) Spider-Man, Thor... I should stop now.

Your next step is to flip over the shuffled cards. Take your visual image you made for each card, and place it along the predetermined course on your path.

For demonstration, I'll give you the nickel tour through my Palace.

My path through this Barnes and Noble store starts at (1) the main entrance. I move clockwise through both floors, starting at the 6:00 position. The path moves to the left, where (2) three stacks of magazines await my perusal. Past that are several locations in (3) the cafe. All this is along the left side of the store.

I then move to the right where the games are, followed by a shelf with Rubik's cube variations.

At the back of the store is the Music/Audio section. I pass through the security gates, on to the left where the Christmas music is.

That's one of my favorite things about these journeys. Is there Christmas music at the B&N right now? Not physically. In mind Memory Palace? Always.

After I leave the music area, I hit the entertainment books, followed by the cards section, the checkout line, and finally up the Escalator. I didn't point them all out, but that covers 26 loci, or half the deck.

I initially worried there wouldn't be enough locations. Now, I could probably fit all 52 cards on either floor, especially if I combine some of the techniques discussed later in the book.

On the top floor, I use the (1) children's section, information desk, kiosk, reference, and education books. Moving clockwise, I go through all the great sections, including fiction, (2) graphic novels, and (3) science fiction. Just past the science fiction books are the (4) romance, and then the (5) erotic books. I use these in my Mind Palace, because they make for vivid images for some of my characters. You should have heard the 9th Doctor explaining what he was looking at, and why.

Finally it's the bathrooms, photography, and then back down the escalator.

One of my favorite images from memorizing cards came in the bathroom area.

The Wampa snow monster (5 of Diamonds) was pounding on the men's bathroom door. Finally it opened to reveal David Tennant as the 10th Doctor (and 10 of Clubs) saying, "I'm sorry. I'm so sorry."

What does your path look like? Before continuing take the time to create one, along with mnemonics for each of the cards. It's the hardest part of the process. I promise.

Another Approach

I mentioned other methods for memorizing cards. Some people may benefit from another point of view. Personally, I read through several explanations before combining techniques into a style all my own. Below you'll find another approach, though all that really changes are the mnemonics. Pick the ones that work best in your mind.

By the way, if the above works for you, then read this next section purely for the writing style. If the writing isn't strong enough for your tastes, then read it for an overview of upcoming systems. (Also, if the latter is true, please don't rate this book.)

If using the Major system, or the PAO system appeals to you, then you're in luck. We'll go into more detail in subsequent chapters on both of those.

Anthony Metivier describes using the Major Method for memorizing cards. If you've enjoyed my tongue-in-cheek self-promotion, then you'll love his memory books. He does the same, without the tongue or cheek.

I kid. I emailed Anthony, prior to putting him in the book. He was more than gracious. His information is solid. Here's how he remembers cards.

The Major system I keep teasing translates numbers into consonant sounds. It goes something like this:

0 = Z, or S. (0 starts with Z, which sounds like S.)

1 = T, or D. (1 is made with a downward stroke like the letters.)

2 = N. (N has two downward strokes.)

3 = M. (M has three downward strokes.)

4 = R. (4 ends in R. This is much easier to remember than I thought.)

5 = L. (L is the Roman numeral for 50. I know, V is the numeral for 5, but we use that later on. If you hold up 5 fingers on your left hand, you'll form an L with your index finger and thumb. Maybe that will help remember.)

6 = CH, and some other sounds I avoid because they're too close to others. (I've kind of just accepted this as a given. But a lower case g does kind of look like a flipped 6.)

7 = K, or Hard G. (K looks similar to two 7s laying on each other.)

8. V, or F. (I've seen a few explanations of why, but I stick with remembering that I should have had a V8.)

9. P, or B. (P looks like 9 flipped. B looks like it's turned 180 degrees.)

This is used for memorizing numbers. Vowels are added, along with any necessary consonant sounds not used in the system. All this forms words, which then form images. 22 might be a nun. 9 by itself could be seen as poo. And so on.

Anthony then assigns a number range for each of the cards. Spades start at 10, Diamonds at 30, Clubs at 50, and Hearts at 80.

After that, you come up with a mnemonic for each of the numbers. You know that the Ace of Spades has a value of 11, so that could be a toad. The 2 of Spades then turns into tin. The 9 of Diamonds could be a map. And so on.

I'm not knocking this method. Learning to translate numbers into sounds, then into images that I'd preassigned to each card just seemed like too much work. However, just like the way I went about it, that's the hardest part of the job.

To limit the number of loci needed for cards, you might also choose to learn a **PA** or **PAO** technique.

I'll cover both of these in more detail shortly. They're pretty easy.

PA stands for Person-Action. Instead of just remembering that the Jack of Diamonds is *Luke Skywalker,* you'd also remember him *swinging a lightsaber.* The 8 of Spades then becomes a *snowman* that is *doing yoga.* Like they do sometimes.

You put it together like this. If your first two cards are the Jack of Diamonds and the 8 of Spades, your first location becomes Luke Skywalker doing yoga. You've just stored two cards in one loci. By the way, let's hope it's young Luke in the yoga poses. I don't think the Force Awakens version could manage.

PAO takes it one more step. Person-Action-Object. Now you assign a person, doing an action, to an object. So now you might picture Luke Skywalker doing yoga on top of a kiss-o-gram worker, assuming the third card was Amy Pond's 3 of Clubs.

The upside is you store more information in one location. The downside is you have to come up with additional actions, and possibly objects, for each card.

Remember to burn the old Palace down before starting again. Also, make sure you realize that Vegas won't let you use your own cards. As fun as remembering cards can be, it has limited value in the casinos.

I've been amazed at how easy this is. It's almost like I don't even see the cards anymore. All I see is River, Clara, Amy.

7. Numbers. Now This Is Major

Remember the scene in Star Wars: Episode I, where Qui-Gon, Obi-Wan, and Jar-Jar Binks are attacked by a gooberfish?

I'm kidding. Of course you don't. The beloved J.J. Abrahms banished all Jar-Jar scenes from the collective memory with Episode VII. Curse this newfound memory. After I finish this book, I think I'm going to write something about how to forget things.

Here's what happens in the scene. Make sure not to put these details in a Memory Palace, or you'll never be able to get them out of your head again.

As the trio left the Gungan city in a submersible vehicle, the giant fish stuck out its frog-like tongue, nabbing the underwater car. All, it seemed, was lost. But then, in a mighty display of CGI, another sea creature known as an opee sea killer came out of nowhere, crunched the gooberfish in its own mighty jaws, and promptly disappeared into the green screen from whence it came.

Our heroes were saved. There was not great rejoicing, because so was Jar-Jar.

The best part of the scene? Qui-Gon remarking that, "There's always a bigger fish."

There's also always a better memory system.

Let's start with one I've already partially introduced, the Major Memory system.

It's not called Major because it's the best, or because it requires a college degree to implement. Why then does it possess such a lofty name?

Here's the part where I wanted to explain it got its name from the creator, some guy called Major. I hadn't written the chapter on remembering names yet, so it seemed justifiable to fact check this.

Turns out Pierre Hérigone came up with it. It says so on Wikipedia. Why isn't it named after him? Simple. That's self-explanatory. Can you imagine trying to learn something called the Hérigone system? We'd need a system just to remember how to pronounce this one.

Then Stanislaus Mink von Wennsshein worked on it some, and that would have been even worse. Let's fast forward a bit. At least six other people with unsatisfactory names got their hands on the system before finally, Major Beniowski wrote a book that included the information on the system.

Memory scholars around the world rejoiced. Finally, they had a name worth remembering, all thanks to Major's book.

I haven't read this book, but I think I almost have to. Wikipedia says it's called *The Anti-Absurd or Phrenotypic English Pronouncing and Orthographical Dictionary*. I can't tell if that's a book, or the first draft of a Steven Moffat script.

Oh, and I have to share this before we get into the major stuff. That book that Wikipedia references? The footnote references a blog post found at blog.artofmemory.com. The blog post references the same Wikipedia article.

Or, as C3P0 said in Episode 2, "How perverse."

Sigh Is there an art of forgetting blog?

Here's a reminder of how the major system works. You assign a letter sound to each number you come across:

0 = Z, or S.
1 = T, or D.
2 = N.
3 = M.
4 = R.
5 = L.
6 = CH, J.
7 = K, or Hard G.
8. V, or F.
9. P, or B.

Here's why it works. Chunking.

Those of you that grew up in the 80's, and remember the Goonies might think means pulling your shirt up to your neck, and wiggling you belly fat while making gibberish noises. I agree that would leave a memorable image. Who could forget the truffle shuffle? Not me, and I'm wanting to learn about how to forget even more now.

Fortunately, the truffle shuffle isn't a memory technique.

Chunking is grouping bits of information together, so you have to remember fewer individual items.

Could you easily remember the number 117412241225? Possibly, but unless you notice a pattern, or already know some techniques, chances are you'd struggle to get past the first 7 or so numbers in the sequence. But what if we simplified it?

Let's chunk 117412241225 and see if it gets easier.

11 - 74 - 1224 - 1225. Is that easier? Well, sure, but it could still prove challenging. Let's associate these numbers with something.

New Years. Independence Day. Christmas Eve. Christmas Day. Could you remember that, now? Almost certainly.

1/1 = New Years. 7/4 = Independence Day. 12/24 = Christmas Eve. 12/25 = Christmas Day.

This is the Major System's basis. Unrelated numbers aren't easily memorized. But, giving them associations that can be quickly translated into numbers is.

How does it work? Let's start simple. Take the number 716157.

Two options for memorizing this number present themselves, depending on what kind of geek tendencies one might possess. If you're the kind that already knows the Klingon language, simply remember this as the Klingon word *K'tChtlk*. Loosely translated, that means, "One who makes stuff up." It's the closest the language comes to our word for *writer*, which is odd, seeing as how proud they are of Shakespeare.

If you *don't* know Klingon, you can turn this into a set of images. 71 becomes KT, which I'd turn into *KITT*. KITT was the black corvette from Knight Rider. It stands for Knight Industries Two Thousand, and I only just now realized how dated that reference sounds.

61 becomes ChT, which could become *cheat*, but unless you're an NFL fan, it could be hard to come up with an image for that. (For those of you into football, just conjure up the New England Patriots.) I love football, but I'm going to go with *cheetah* instead. Yes, it has the consonant 'h,' but that's not part of the system, so it's fair game. Unlike deflated footballs.

57 is LK, so it forms the image of a *leak*.

Put it together, adding it to a Memory Palace, and you might have KITT doing donuts on your dining room table, an anthropomorphic cheetah washing dishes at your sink, and even though it makes no sense, water gushing out of that leak in your microwave.

It's not imperative to use the Major System with a Memory Palace, but I'd recommend it if the goal is to remember multiple numbers for a long period of time.

The system works. I use it to memorize my travel itineraries when I fly.

Remember that it's better to picture a person, place, or thing than it is to picture a concept. The image for 04 could be worked out as sorrow. How would that be pictured? Sure, the picture a sad face crying could be conjured. But when you come back to the image, will you think it stood for *sorrow, crying, tears, sad, or sadness*? Those would give you completely different numbers — 06, 72, 10, 01, and 0120 respectively.

Here are a few suggestions to get started. Note that single digits like 6 produce a different number than 06, because the zero must be accounted for.

0 - Sea.

1 - Toe.

2 - Noah.

3 - Emma. (If you know anyone named *Emma,* use that. I do. If not, try *home.*)

4 - Roo. (From Winnie the Poo. Guess what number nine is going to be?)

5 - Loo. (I picture a toilet. This image could also be for the number 151, but I know which one I mean.)

6 - Shoe.

7 - Cow.

8 - Wave.

9 - Poo. (Either picture Winnie the Poo, or... you know.)

10 - DOS. I'm a computer guy, so I picture a *DOS* screen. If that makes no sense to you, try the word *daisy.*

01 - Soda.

02 - Sun.

03 - Sumo.

04 - Sarah. I also know a *Sarah.* If you don't, I'm not sure what to tell you. This is a hard image for me to come up with non-concept related images. You could also try *Hoosier,* or *Swearing.*

05 - Seal.
06 - Sushi. Especially spicy tuna rolls. Mmmm.
07 - Sock.
08 - Sofa. (Remember that 8 uses a V or an F.)
09 - Soup.
11 - Dad.
22 - Nun.
33 - Mom.
44 - Roar. (A standalone verb is almost as bad as a concept, because you might think it's the verb, or the thing doing the verb. If it's not at the start of a number you're memorizing, you can make the item before it roar. So, if you're learning 0744, picture a *Cow Roaring*.
55 - Hallelujah. (For instance, picture a choir singing the Hallelujah chorus.)
66 - Shush.
77 - Coke.
88 - Good luck with this one. Possible words include *five, Fauve, fief, Fife, FIFO, viva*, and *vive*. And if you choose the first one in that list, you're crazy.
99 - Puppy.

Want to practice? Good.

Just a couple of nights ago, I helped out a friend with a computer problem. Among other things, the computer needed more memory. That feels like it should be funny, but it's not. I helped order the memory online, and she gave me her credit card to place the order.

She said I was one of the only people she trusted with her card, which was good, because I proceeded to demonstrate my newfound skills by reciting the card number back to her. Full disclosure. I didn't memorize the CVC number, or the expiration date. Neither did I commit the images to a long term Memory Palace, so the number is already gone. (In other words, if that card becomes involved in identity theft, or credit card fraud, it's not my fault.)

In case you're wondering, there's all kinds of practical uses too. I travel. A lot. Generally, I haven't needed much help remembering my hotel numbers. Without realizing I was doing it, I used a form of the loci method, picturing the location of my room. In conjunction with repeating the room number to myself over and over, I used to be able to remember the number, almost without fail.

Almost. My travel schedule keeps me moving, and sometimes the hotels, locations, and numbers ran together.

I still visualize the location of my room. But tonight, as I'm writing this from inside the hotel room, I can still see a taser zapping anybody that walks past my door.

Taser. TZR. 104.

Another night, I found myself in room 490. That became RIPS in the carpet in front of my room.

Would I remember these numbers without this mnemonic? Probably. Will I forget them while I'm on the trips? Definitely not.

We use computers, notepads, and smart phones to remember the myriad of numbers we encounter every day. That method works until a phone gets lost, or the robot apocalypse breaks out. Why leave something like that to chance?

Now for your practice. In the days before cell phones, it was common practice to remember phone numbers. You couldn't just look on your phone for the person's name. Why? No screens.

Phone numbers here in the states have 10 digits. How many of these random 10 digit numbers can you memorize? (And please note, I just used a random number generator to come up with these. As far as I know, none of these correspond to real numbers. Just in case, please don't go calling these people. If anyone answers, I doubt they'd appreciate it. But if you do call and make a friend, mention this book to them, okay?)

4356983886
1531986376
5235110605
3707236352
9790266840

There. Now you've finished a major section of this book. Shortly, we'll move on to PAO, which puts this system to shame. Or, as Qui-Gon said, "There's always a bigger fish."

8. PAO and Dominic

Ever heard of the World Memory Championships?

It's where mental athletes across the world compete in the world's greatest test of memory.

Chances are, you'll never see these athletes on SportCenter's Top Ten Plays. And if you do, you can bet that it's Baseball season. That doesn't mean memory athlete's accomplishments aren't impressive. They just don't make for great television.

Watching people with their eyes closed, taping their heads, and reciting numbers all day vs an extra inning mid-season baseball game. Meh. Let's see what's new on Netflix.

One of the events held at these memory championships is the 5 Minute Number. Contestants are given 5 minutes to memorize as many numbers as possible, then another 15 minutes to recall them. In this event, somebody once recounted 395 numbers during this time. Impressive? Oh, yes. But it's still not good enough to be one of the top ten best times in these events.

As of this writing, the five hundred mark has been broken at least three times in this event.

The Major system isn't likely to get someone near those kinds of numbers. There's simply too many images to store. It'd be like trying to look into the heart of the time vortex. Even if a memory championship isn't the goal, the efficiency of this next method warrants the effort involved to learn it.

As I said before, there's a bigger fish.

PAO, or Person-Action-Object, stuffs more information into a single image. With it, you can memorize three different items into a single section of memory. This is typically used in memorizing numbers or cards, though it can be implemented to remember other things, like poetry. For now, we're going to stick to numbers and cards.

Here's the small downside. This system takes some work to get started, but once you've put in the time, the number of items you can store grows by a factor of three. I think that's right, anyway. This is a memory book, not mathematics.

The great thing about PAO, and every other system in this book for that matter, is it can (and should) be sculpted to work for you. This particular system is especially geared to personalizing the objects.

Pick what works best. We're going to explore three possibilities to use in a PAO system— Major, Dominic, and Arbitrary. While not an exhaustive list, those three variations are more than enough to get started with an informed decision. For starters, we're going to look at the Major system again.

PAO assigns a *Person* performing an *Action*, on a particular *Object*.

Using Major mnemonics, we said 22 could be a nun. That's the person in the PAO. The action could be making the sign of the cross, and the object could be over the heart.

11 represented Dad. The action might be hammering. The object could be a nail.

03 was a sumo wrestler. So here, the action might be falling, and the object would be a wrestling ring.

So, when trying to remember a sequence of numbers that includes 221103, it would be broken down into 22-11-03. The only image needed for this would be a nun hammering a wrestling ring.

Several people combine the major Method with PAO. So many in fact, I'd be remiss not to start with this one.

It doesn't work for me. I use the Major method for small numbers just fine. Personally, it's difficult enough coming up with images for each number, let alone a person, action, and object for all of them. Fortunately there are (at least) two other alternatives.

Dominic O'Brien developed the Dominic system, because he always wanted something named after him.

Part of that last sentence may not be true. But consider this. Dominic says that *Dominic* stands for *Decipherment of Mmemonically Interpreted Numbers Into Characters*. One can only assume if he'd been named Robb, we'd have something called the *Remembering Objects By Brevity System*.

It works similarly to the Major encoding. Instead of assigning sounds to each digit number, a letter is assigned instead. This difference may appear negligible, but many people find it much easier to create images using these letters. Also, the letters are easier to remember in Dominic.

Here are the details:

1 = A
2 = B
3 = C
4 = D
5 = E
6 = S
7 = G
8 = H
9 = N
0 = O

See? That only looks a little arbitrary. 1-5 correspond to the letter's position in the alphabet, as do 7 and 8. 6 starts with an S sound. 8 and H sound similar. 9 has the N sound, and for years people have openly wondered, "Is that supposed to be an O or a 0?" Now the answer is, of course, "Yes."

Using these letters makes it easy to come up with images on the fly, but to fully maximize Dominic for Person-Action-Object, preassign a PAO for each 2 digit sequence, from 00 - 99.

Here's what that looks like.

67 might be Supergirl firing heat vision at a mirror. The person is *Supergirl*, the action, *heat vision*, and the *mirror* is the object. Notice that the abbreviation SG only applies to the name.

The goal isn't to picture Supergirl doing this every time you have to memorize a sequence of numbers including 67. Well, not unless the number is 676767. And after all, she's going to run out of mirrors pretty quickly that way.

15 might be Albert Einstein sticking out his tongue at a camera.

63 would be Sean Connery shaking a martini.

Using Dominic with PAO, we encode all those numbers into one image. 671563 = 67-15-63. That easily becomes one image of Supergirl sticking out her tongue at a martini.

Parsing the order of numbers out of this image is easy, because it's always Person-Action-Object.

When assigning PAO combinations, start with numbers that already have strong associations. Ignore the number-letter assignments for those, and go with the pre-existing images.

For instance, if 23 makes you think of Michael Jordan, clearly you're a basketball fan with fond memories of the game. This image will work better than Bryan Cranston.

03 for me would probably be Spock, because Star Trek 3 was the search for Spock. He'd probably be mind-melding with a rock. Or maybe VGer, but that would remind me of *The Motionless Picture*.

That's just me. The classics don't work as well for others. Someone right now might very well be thinking, "Hey, Rosie Huntington-Whiteley was in the third Transformers movie. I'll just imagine her, doing whatever she did in that movie, to whatever she did it to."

If that someone is you, shame on you. Not for thinking of Rosie, but for giving Michael Bay more money to make garbage movies. He fooled me once with Transformers, but fortunately I saw it at the dollar theater. Somehow, he fooled me again with Revenge of The Fallen. "No more," I said. Right there in the theater, too. You've never heard so many movie goers shushing me.

Rosie Huntington-Whiteley? Frankly, I had to look up who was in the third film. I had no idea.

Even so, I still love it when a movie trailer says something like, "From Michael Bay," or, "From the creators of Teenage Mutant Ninja Turtles (2014.)" Those are shortcuts that let me know, *I'm never watching this film.* Just like these memorization techniques, that can be a great time saver.

Once the list of numbers with strong connotations has been completed, fill in the gaps using the abbreviations of names.

Full disclosure. I didn't like the first series of NuWho until somewhere around "The Doctor Dances." Up until then, I would alternate with an episode of the 10th Doctor, and then go back to watch an episode of the 9th. Wait, that's not what I meant to say.

I don't use Dominic. Not yet, anyway. I'm still working on coming up with my own 100 images. As of right now, I'm only using PAO for cards, which means I don't need 100 PAO combinations. 52 is more than enough, and most of the work had already been paved. I plan to put in the work to finish my Dominic system soon, because it feels like the best of these three approaches.

Some people also assign what seems like completely arbitrary images to their numbers.

Just like with Dominic, pick numbers that already have strong connotations. Then, come up with other images, and memorize them. Because they're images, this will be easier than it appears at first.

For instance, it may sound a tad crazy to assign 55 to an image of Luna Lovegood, but with a little bit of time and practice, the images will stick.

The images seem random, but with some thought, they'll make sense to the person who comes up with the system. Just like every time I see King of Spade, or the Queen of Diamonds, I immediately form an image that makes perfect sense to me.

I already had 52 images. Not all of them were *Persons*, but with some work, they converted quite nicely.

Here are just a few examples, and some problems I had to solve.

2 of Clubs:

This card was the Tardis. That's not a person. Or is it? Neil Gaiman (*may-he-write-forever*) is one of the greatest writers of this, or any, time. He wrote a Doctor Who Episode called, "The Doctor's Wife," where the Tardis turns into a person. Well, its personality was absorbed into a person named Idris. Finally, we learned the reason the Tardis doesn't always take the Doctor where he wants to go is that she's taking him where he needs to go. That explains a lot of plots.

In this episode, she helps build another Tardis out of spare parts. One hopes this Tardis never turns into a person. If it does though, I hope Neil writes the story about the Frankenstein Tardis.

This chapter is threatening to get away from me.

The 2 of Clubs is the anthropomorphic Tardis (Idris) putting together spare Tardis parts.

5 of Diamonds:

The Wampa monster gnawing on a dead Tauntaun.

Q of Clubs:

River Song writing in her time journal.

5 of Hearts:

I didn't share my hearts before. There's a metaphor for a Time Lord. This card is my dog, Reecee, barking at the door.

7 of Spades:

The spades needed major overhauling. Pun intended. Almost none of them worked as persons. Where I needed to, I replaced them with Star Trek Images. The only real question was which card to use for 7 of 9. Her image is 7 of 9 singing *You Are My Sunshine*.

A of Diamonds:

Oddly, the Death Star still works for me as a person. So this image is the Death Star firing a giant laser beam of destruction at a planet.

Put all these together, and they become two images. The first the **2 of Clubs**, the **5 of Diamonds**, and the **Queen of Clubs**. This image is the anthropomorphic Idris gnawing on a time journal. The next set of cards is the **5 of Hearts**, **7 of Spades**, and the **Ace of Diamonds**. That's visualized as Reecee singing about a planet.

Here's something to remember when starting PAO. Its power is in its efficiency. One single image contains all the information needed for three items. With my new system, I can see the Ninth Doctor shooting force lighting at C3PO's red arm, and know instantly the next three cards are the 9 of Clubs, King of Diamonds and the 3 of Diamonds.

All of this should be quicker to encode in memory than before, as well as to retrieve. That's exactly the case. Eventually.

Prior to learning PAO, I was memorizing a single deck of cards without error within anywhere from five to eight minutes. That wasn't nearly good enough to challenge anyone in a memory competition, but it more than met my needs.

After procrastinating my development of a PAO system for cards, I finally sat down and figured out a Person-Action-Object for every card. Some cards had to change. Instead of a Sonic Screwdriver for the Ace of Clubs, I substituted Rose Tyler with her eyes (the object) glowing (the action. The Spades became Star Trek characters, like the Borg Queen blowing on arm hair for the Queen. What's worked out the best is the Jack. This is represented by Riker shaving his beard. That's led to great images as the card characters keep shaving really weird objects.

Thrilled to see how much better my memory had grown, I raced to memorize another deck. I lost track of how many mistakes I made, which doesn't even include the images I couldn't find in my Palace at all.

The right kind of practice made this all better. Here's what I discovered.

Be sure of the PAO images. I drilled myself on each of the suits. Then, I shuffled the deck, and without memorizing, I went through each PAO combination of each randomly shuffled card.

Finally, I shuffled again and memorized. Everything flowed smoother, but I still made mistakes. It took me a couple more shuffles to realize the problem. I was remembering Kirk (Ace of Spades) sleeping (7 of Hearts) with a miniature planet as his pillow (Ace of Diamonds.) But remembering isn't the same as seeing the image in the mind's eye. After making sure of the images, I spent time truly constructing the images. Only after all that could my previous success be matched and surpassed.

Put together, that's a lot to absorb and learn. It doesn't all have to be done at once. Give it time. The more practice and time spent on these, the easier it all becomes.

Don't let the enormity of 100 images become overwhelming. And don't let it keep you from learning more. In fact, I bet you can already face the next challenge.

9. Name That Face (Or, How I Learned To Care. Sort Of)

I still read comic books. Sometimes.

Used to be, before I moved away from this particular city, I'd frequent the same comic book shop about once every 2-3 weeks.

The owner was nice. He'd always say "Hello," and could talk to customers about more than just comic book lore. He even knew my name. That impressed me, since it's something I'd always struggled with. Not remembering my own name, I mean. Remembering others.

I moved, which meant I stopped going by the shop.

A little over five years later, I moved back to the same city. A few months after that, I decided to drop by the shop.

I've since learned that the owner's name was Chris, though I hadn't known that during my previous visits.

I walked into the shop for the first time in maybe six years.

Chris looked up from the book he was reading, nonchalantly said, "Oh, hey Scott," and went back to reading.

If I'd been a silver age comic book hero, an exclamation mark followed by a question mark would have hovered over my head. Also, I would've have had a cape, and probably been able to fly.

How'd he do that? I never asked, but I bet it has something to do with this story.

This is the story of Leah, Matthew, Colleen, Donna, Derrick, and Caitlin. There are others, but these were the first. The story starts with a joke. It's a variation on an old joke, but I've used it every chance I get.

Humor me. It's the last time I get to make the joke.

An unsuspecting friend asks me if I know somebody.

"Probably," I say.

"What do you mean, 'probably?'"

"I might know him, but I'm horrible with names. It's so bad."

"Yeah?" the friend asks. "How bad is it?"

I pretend to ponder the question, before saying, "Hmm. What's that feeling you get when you're really, REALLY happy?"

"Um... delighted?"

"No," I say. "It's shorter than that. Like, happy, happy — what's the word? When you're jumping for something?"

"Oh," the friend says. "You mean joy?"

I slap my hands. "Yes! Joy! Thank you. Just today, I was telling my wife, Joy, that I'm horrible at remembering names."

Unfortunately, I either have to pretend I'm still bad at this, or learn a new joke.

Here's what I'm not going to tell you to do. Repeat the person's name over and over and over again. That's the most common advice I've come across for remembering names, but there's a couple of problems with that.

First, repeating the name doesn't associate it with something. Yes, you'll have a better chance of remembering that name later in the conversation. What happens three weeks from now when you see the person again?

And secondly, it gets awkward.

Imagine this conversation:

"Hi, I'm Scott. And you are?"

"Isabella."

"Well, it is a pleasure to meet you, Isabella."

"Thanks. Is this your first time here?"

"Ha! No, Isabella, I come here all the time. This is the first time I've seen you here, I think."

"I'm sure I wouldn't know."

"That makes sense, Isabella. Guess you see a lot of people come through, eh?"

She sighs. "All day, every day."

"Does it ever get to you, Isabella?"

"Listen, Scott, I've got tons of orders to put in. Do you know what you want to eat or not?"

"...I need a minute."

"Take your time." She makes a beeline towards the kitchen where she tells the manager, "That creepy, stalker guy that repeats our names is back."

If you must repeat the person's name, go ahead. Once. Maybe do it again, like you normally would during a regular conversation. Anything beyond that? Keep it to yourself.

What I'm about to share with you works. Sounds like I'm a snake oil salesman, or an infomercial doesn't it? Sorry about that. It excites me, is all. Maybe not to the level of a Star Wars teaser trailer. But it's still big.

Just today, I met a customer. He came into the room for about thirty seconds, and left. Three hours later, I ran into him as he was leaving the work location. I gave him a firm handshake, and said, "It was great meeting you, Mike."

It'd be funnier if his name turned out to be Fredrick after all. Alas, I got it right on the first try.

Before learning these techniques, I wouldn't have dared trying that.

The method I use for remembering names is borrowed and adapted from a memory champion known as Ron White. When Ron performs memory demonstrations, he will meet people prior to his talk. Then, when he speaks in front of the group, he goes down the rows, telling people their names. He has done this with up to 301 people.

Impressive. Contrast this with me. I've literally known some people in social and work circles for years, and never learned their names. At some point around year three, it becomes too late to admit that, "I never caught your name. Would you mind repeating it for me?"

(If you're reading this book, have known me for years, and can never recall me actually addressing you by name — then you know who you are. Even if I don't.)

Like remembering cards, numbers, lists, and more, there are many visualization techniques to commit names to memory. The thing I liked most about Ron's technique, is it revealed my biggest obstacle. I can explain it best with another bit of Doctor Who dialog, while also giving kudos to my wife.

Doctor: This is Clara, not my assistant... some other word.
Clara: I'm his carer.
Doctor: Yeah, my carer. She cares so I don't have to.

My wife is my carer too. I don't care enough. Certainly not enough to remember people's names.

(If you're reading this book, have known me for years, and can never recall me actually addressing you by name, this doesn't mean I don't care enough about you. Well— not necessarily.)

Some people are extroverts. They have outgoing personalities, and engage with others. They need social interaction.

Some people are introverts. They are generally more reserved. They can be around other people, but they have to withdraw for a period to recharge.

Some time back a Myers-Briggs test showed that, among other things, I am about 50% extrovert, and 50% introvert. I think that's called an ambivert.

Some who know me might be surprised. They see me feeding off of crowds, engaging and interacting with people. I draw attention to myself. I entertain. I love people.

Well...

More self-reflection, here. This is getting back to names. I promise.

I love... individuals. Some of them, anyway. Other individuals I merely like. But people? In groups? I love their attention. I love it when they are focused on me. I love being in crowds when I can be noticed. Otherwise, they just drain the life out of me.

I'm not a narcissist, but I can kind of see the appeal.

As much as I enjoy interacting with people, I often have to withdraw. I have to find some time alone.

Some people can't stand the thought of eating alone. I can't stand the thought of eating alone without a book.

For years, this approach to people prevented me from learning their names.

I didn't care enough when I initially met them to learn their names. Later, when I did care enough about the individual, it was often too late to ask. All I could do was hope I'd hear someone else say the name, then hope I could remember it later. I rarely did remember, because I didn't have a method. I do now, and it starts with caring.

But don't worry, Joy. You still get to be my carer when it doesn't involve names.

Ron's first step to name memorization is to focus on the person. I think of it as caring. I have to care enough to learn their name. I find it out, by listening, reading a name tag, or if all else fails, by asking them. This feels shameful to admit, but one of the things I've learned from memorizing is to see people as individuals.

The second step is to choose the most outstanding feature of the person, typically on their face. This has to be a feature you will notice every time you see the person. Do Jenny's glasses jump out at you? Feel free to focus on them, as long as you're sure she doesn't occasionally wear contacts. Does her facial hair draw your attention? It sure would mine. Ask her if she's likely to shave her face, and if not, that's the obvious choice.

When I'm meeting people now, I'm reminding myself to find out their name, and (hopefully discreetly) studying their features to discover the most outstanding feature.

Possibilities include bushy hair, prominent freckles, bald heads, deep eyes, Peter-Capaldi-like-eyebrows, beards, double-chins, big cheeks, unique noses, and so on. If your eyes are drawn towards it, that's what you want to focus on. This will be the trigger for your memory to pull the name out of your mind's recesses.

Here's where I begin to differ from Ron, in that I turn his next two steps into a single one. The end result is the same, a memorable image that vividly brings a name to mind.

Our minds are designed to remember images better than names. That's why most of us have an easier time recalling faces. The next step is to create an image that reminds you of the person's name.

A few guidelines. First, you're going to repeat these images for people with the same names. If an ant drawing the person's features is your image for Andrew (Ant-Draw = Andrew) then every Andrew you meet will have that same image. The location may vary, based on whether you're focusing on Andrew's pencil-thin mustache, or his uni-brow, but it's still an ant drawing Andrew's prominent features.

Make this image clear. Al *might* be remembered as something saying, "Ow," but that's not very clear is it? But, if you use *owl* instead, that's an easy visualization to make.

Also, be sure the image is doing something. Put it into action. You might not remember the owl if it's just perched on Al's head. If the owl is dive bombing into Al's head, that's an image that's hard to forget.

Try to avoid using other people's names for your images. Unless, of course, the person is so iconic or memorable, that you just can't help it. I actually met an Adolph once. This was before I learned these techniques, but somehow, I've never had any problems remembering his name.

If you meet a Wanda, picturing your Aunt Wanda as a face on your new co-worker's mole is likely to confuse you. If a wand protrudes out of her mole, casting miniaturization spells on everything in sight, the image is more likely to stick.

That reminds me. Don't tell anyone that every time you see them, you imagine a magical wand protruding from their mole. That's no way to make friends. I learned that my first day trying this out.

Combine the image with the feature you notice first. I'll provide some more examples, but first, let's review the last step.

Go over what you've learned. Before you finish your day, review the people you've met. You might even want to write them down, at least at first.

So far, I haven't had any problems remembering the new names I've learned. I haven't built a Memory Palace for names yet, because I haven't decided how I want to organize them.

If I were starting a new job, (Hey, Boss. I'm not planning to do that any time soon) I'd definitely build a Palace of the new location, and put my coworkers' names in the places they actually work.

As it stands, I'd finally learned most everybody's name at my main work location, minus a couple of the new people. And I've since used this technique for learning the new ones.

Remembering everyone's name at work isn't that hard. Want to know how many people work at my job? Nearly half of them. (Just kidding.)

All that said, if you don't review, you will forget. So review at the end of the day, or the end of the week.

That's the method. Want some numbered steps? Happy to oblige.

1) **Care** - Learn the name(s.)

2) **Feature** - Find the most eye drawing feature.

3) **Image** - Create a mnemonic image that interacts with that feature.

4) **Remember** - File the new names away, in a notebook, a Memory Palace, or simply by running through the names in your head.

Here are some examples I've used already.

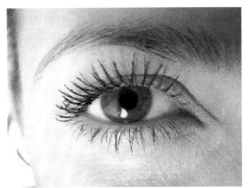

Image by Michael Sandoval and used under an
Attribution –ShareAlike 2.0 License
https://www.flickr.com/photos/do-it_do-it-now/

I took my two daughters out to eat. Our waitress identified herself as Leah. Leah had long eyelashes that drew all attention towards her eyes. Every time she came to our table, I imagined her eyelashes were living trees, thrashing their limbs and yelling "Yah! Yah! Yah!" at everybody. *Tree-Yah* = Leah.

Shortly before we left, I asked my oldest daughter if she remembered the waitress's name. Much to my dismay, she did.

At a Starbucks, Matthew took my order. His bushy eyebrows seemed to follow me, despite which way he focused his gaze. Matthew = *Matt Pew.* I visualized a church pew made out of place mats. Anytime someone sat in the mats, they fell apart.

At Barnes & Noble, I met a Colleen. She sported a long and slightly bent nose. I wouldn't have necessarily noticed it if I hadn't been looking for something to focus on. When I did, it jumped out at me. It nearly gouged me. I decided on the spot that *calling* sounded like Colleen. An old fashioned telephone, with the twisted cord attached to the handset, fell out of her nose. A tiny person hung to the other end of it, frantically trying to make a call. Poor Colleen. She'd be almost cute, if she didn't have a tiny elfish creature hanging from her nose.

Donna = *llama*. A llama munches on her curly hair every time I see her. This is why I can't tell people what their images are. It's also why I hope Donna doesn't buy this book.

Derrick's hair is prematurely balding. Well, I'm assuming it's premature. Either way, I remember his name by seeing a deer licking his forehead. Don't tell him either, okay? *Deer lick* = Derrick.

Caitlin taught me to pay even more attention to people. She was another waitress. When she came to our table with our tea, I asked her to, "Settle a bet. Did you say your name was Caitlin or Kathleen?" I was sure it was Kathleen, because I saw a cat leaning against her curly hair. The cat purred, and nearly fell off our waitresses' head because it leaned over so far.

She said it was "Caitlin," and I groaned. Now I had to come up with the image of a gate with a giant hen crashing through it, and getting tangled in Caitlin's hair. *Gate Hen* = Caitlin. I liked the other image better, but our waitress wasn't interested in changing her name. I tipped her anyway.

Now, I know what you're thinking. You're thinking, "No, you don't. You're my new most favorite writer ever, but even you couldn't possibly know what I'm thinking."

But prior to that, you just might have been wondering how to apply this technique to twins.

That's easy. Fortunately, in addition to outstanding taste in geek cultural references, I also happen to *be a twin*. Here's how I'd apply the technique in our situation.

I'd know that my image for Scott would apply to the male twin, and my image for Stacey would apply to the female twin.

See? It's helpful tidbits like this one, that make this book such an invaluable resource.

10. Fifty States of Mind

There are so many more techniques, methods, and systems to explore. I haven't even scratched the surface. Did you know you can have a Palace within a Palace?

My attic door has a poster board on it. My youngest daughter drew a picture of The Doctor's Tardis on it. All I have to do is open the door, discover my Palace is bigger on the inside, and I'm in an entirely different world. A world, full of locations I remember, and can place memories in.

I can have picture books on a table, with pictures that suck me into more Palaces. Bookshelves with books, all of them another Palace. A hidden doorway that leads to the woods I played in as a child. That wardrobe in my attic? You can bet it's a door to Narnia.

And that's just the Palaces.

Ever have problems remembering directions? For that matter, do you remember having to remember directions, back before Google Maps?

Some of my travels have taken me to places without cellular service. There are ways to navigate in this world without cell service. If you have enough advance warning, and enough room on the phone, it's not too hard to download offline maps. It is hard to use them if the cell battery dies.

Another way is to link directions together.

You're lost. You stop at a gas station and ask for directions.

"Simple," the cashier says. "Take the third left on Onteora Boulevard. At the stop sign turn right onto Bowling Green Avenue. Take the next right at the Starbucks, and go to the end of the road. You can't miss it."

If you already have a Memory Palace set up for temporary information, it's easy.

You can use any of the number memorization methods we've discussed, along with some other visuals.

The third left becomes a set of handcuffs. Handcuffs look like the number three, remember? What about Onteora? The Onte sounds like Auntie. Put an image of your aunt with a pair of handcuffs on her left hand. For the next turn, imagine someone rolling a bowling ball into a stop sign. End up with shooting stars drinking coffee.

Mostly we've discussed how to memorize things. Now it's time for you the explore things worth memorizing.

I cleared out my first Palace of cube colors, to make way for more permanent information. Poems, Scripture, trivia, and information I should know.

All 50 U.S. States and their capitals? Child's play. As a matter of fact, because I learned them with the Memory Palace technique, it's just as easy to rattle them off in reverse order (Z-A) as it is alphabetical order. To go the other direction, all that is required is going through the Palace from the end to the beginning. The images are still there. It took some time to find the right images to trigger the information. I had no idea what a Juneau, Alaska looks like, but now I know it's my wife in a wedding dress sitting inside an igloo.

I promise to explain that in just a minute.

Learn whatever you want. How about a repository for super important dates in history? Like the Louisiana Purchase, the moon landing, and the first airing of David Tennant as The Doctor.

The sky's not the limit anymore.

This book has given a handful of examples for memorizing items. It's steered away from a ton of examples, because the person memorizing needs to have an image that resonates with them.

I doubt I'll ever attempt a memory championship, because I take too long to decide what those images should be. It took a couple of hours to come up with images for the 50 States and the capitals. The actual memorization only took a few minutes.

Before wrapping things up, I'll share the images with you. Hopefully it helps someone. Some of them are going to be meaningful to me.

Full disclosure. Many of these are adapted from this website: http://mrsjonesroom.com/themes/usa.html

- **Alabama - Montgomery**
  An anthropomorphic mountain is blowing bubbles with gum (Mount-Gum = Montgomery,) while on top an owl is eating a huge banana. (Owl-Banana = Alabama.)

- **Alaska - Juneau**
  My wife and I were married in the month of June. So I picture her in her wedding dress, saying that it is Co-o-o-l-d. She is prolonging the O. (June-O = Juneau.) The reason she is cold, is she's inside that igloo, which reminds me of Alaska.

- **Arizona - Phoenix**
  Jean Grey, of Marvel Comics and the X-Men movies, became the Dark Phoenix. So, I see her in attack mode (Phoenix) being shot by an arrow (Arrow = Arizona.) Incidentally, it's Hawkeye firing the arrow. That has nothing to do with Phoenix, Arizona, but it makes me smile at the thought of an X-Men/Avengers live action movie crossover.

- **Arkansas - Little Rock**
  Noah's Ark (Ark = Arkansas) is being pelted by people throwing little rocks (Little Rocks = Little Rock.) Noah wasn't taking them anyway, but he definitely won't know that they've scratched up his brand new boat.

- **California - Sacramento**
  I have a friend from California named Cari. (Cari = California.) She is carrying a sack of tomatoes. (Sack of Tomatoes=Sacramento.)

- **Colorado - Denver**
  My image for this is just too weird to explain. Not that
  I'm shy about sharing my weird, but it also would
  make zero sense. Instead, the Mrs. Jones website says to
  imagine you've painted your den red (Color Red =
  Colorado,) and the walls are made out of fur. (Den Fur
  = Denver.)

- **Connecticut - Hartford**
  Khan, the one from Star Trek II: The Wrath of Khan, is
  holding a bird so tightly, its cartoon heart is visibly
  pumping against its chest. (Khan = UConn =
  Connecticut. Heart = Hartford.)

- **Delaware - Dover**
  Mrs. Jones says to ask, "What did Della wear?" And
  then to answer "She wore doe fur." I try to avoid giving
  images names of things I need to remember if I don't
  already have an image for that person. So I changed
  this to "What does Bella (From Twilight- and don't
  judge me for knowing that) wear?" And to actually see
  her wearing a doe's fur skin, complete with a doe's
  head. And the doe is Bambi's mom. I think if Edward
  left her again, that's just the type of thing Bella might
  do.

- **Florida - Tallahassee**
  This one's easy. In my Memory Palace, it happens to
  take place on my couch. A Seminole, which is the
  mascot of Florida State in Tallahassee, is sitting on the
  couch, watching the game with a Gator- the University
  of Florida. My in-laws would be proud.

- **Georgia - Atlanta**
  I see a miniature scale version of the Atlanta airport,
  complete with a Georgia peach flying around it.

- **Hawaii - Honolulu**
  A Hawaiian girl is dancing at a luau. With a hula hoop. This image works in my head, for some reason.

- **Idaho - Boise**
  A potato (which reminds me of Idaho) with arms and legs is hoeing the field. Hoe also sounds like Idaho.) For some reasons, a few boys are watching the potato. (Boys see = Boise.)

- **Illinois - Springfield**
  The Simpsons are from Springfield. What's more, they are bouncing on springs, and the motion is making them ill. (Ill = Illinois)

- **Indiana - Indianapolis**
  Bobby Knight coached college basketball at Indiana, while wearing those horrid red sweaters. Peyton Manning played for The Indianapolis Colts, wearing a Colts uniform. I imagine the two of them shouting at each other. Knight screams something to him like, "It's @^@&*# basketball, not ^&%&@% football!" Manning, for some reason, just yells back, "Blue 52! Omaha! Omaha!"

- **Iowa - Des Moines**
  This one is convoluted. It's very similar to what Mrs. Jones described, but I'm not sure my image is any less weird. It works for me, which is what counts. I owe (I owe = Iowa) Day Coins (Day Coins = Des Moines.) I've decided that Day Coins are quarters you use in the morning. To further illustrate this, a Rooster knocks at the door, cock-a-doodling, and informing me he'll pluck my feathers out if I don't pay up. In my Memory Palaces, roosters don't know the difference between feathers and hair.

- **Kansas - Topeka**
  I love this image. It happens to take place in my bedroom and on my bed. Dorothy, who isn't in Kansas anymore, is laying on the bed. A sheet covers her from her neck down to her feet, but her toes are peeking out. (Toes peeking = Topeka.) I tried to describe this image to my wife. I told her, "Even though Dorothy stays in our bed in my Mind Palace—" and she stopped me, saying, "There's some images you should just keep to yourself."
- **Kentucky - Frankfort**
  Rick Pitino used to coach Kentucky basketball. He also coached the Boston Celtics, but he's never going to be remembered as the face of that franchise. I imagine him, trying to climb his way into a fort made of hot dogs. (Hot dogs = Franks. Add Franks to fort, and you get Frankfort.)

- **Louisiana - Baton Rouge**
  I have a pretty clear image of Louisiana as a boot. I then imagine Nicole Kidman, as she appeared in Moulin Rouge, sitting on the boot. Moulin Rouge = Baton Rouge.

- **Maine - Augusta**
  This one is straight out of the website I keep referencing. There's a gust of wind (a gust of wind = Augusta) blowing a lion's mane. (Mane = Maine.)

- **Maryland - Annapolis**
  I love Christmas. Growing up, like many families, we had a manger scene that sat on the piano or the coffee table. I see a larger version of Mary from that set (Mary = Maryland,) fishing. It's a special pole, with a huge apple on the line for bait. (An apple pole = Annapolis.)

- **Massachusetts - Boston**
  Unlike Rick, Larry Bird is remembered as the iconic
  face of the Boston Celtic's franchise. (Unless you're old
  enough to remember Bill Russel playing, or young
  enough to see Kevin Garnett, Paul Pierce, or Ray Allen
  as the face. Even if you're young enough for that,
  shame on you. They were great, but they weren't Larry
  Legend. His image is stored at the sink in my
  bathroom. He has a huge mass of chewing tobacco that
  he's spitting into the sink. (Mass of Chew =
  Massachusetts. Larry = Boston.)

- **Michigan - Lansing**
  If Celtic fans don't like the image above, just think how
  Michigan fans will take this one. A huge lance, which is
  like a spear, juts out of a cabinet. It lances Chris
  Webber, who is so flummoxed by what is happening,
  that he calls time-out. (Lance = Lansing. Webber =
  Michigan.) And by the way, Michigan fans, Webber
  traveled after grabbing that rebound. Then, he was
  surrounded by Carolina players, on the sideline, with
  nowhere to pass. No way would Michigan have scored,
  even if he hadn't called the timeout they didn't have.
  UNC was already up by two, and would have gotten
  the ball to seal the game with 11 seconds left. And deep
  down, every single one of you knows it. (Derald, I
  really, *really* hope you're reading this. Go Heels!)
- **Minnesota - St. Paul**
  I imagine a pastor preaching from one of Paul's letters.
  Paul often called the people he wrote to at the churches
  saints, so the pastor is pointing out how the word *saint*
  doesn't refer to super-Christians, or dead people. My
  image is the pastor explaining this (St Paul,) but he's
  also super thirsty. So, he hydrates himself with mini
  soda cans. (Mini Soda = Minnesota.)

- **Mississippi - Jackson**
  All I really have to do is hear Jerry Clower say he is
  from "Jackson, Mississippi." If you remember Jerry, this
  works for you too. If not, check him out on YouTube,
  and in the meantime, picture kids playing jacks in the
  Mississippi. This could be the river, or the state.

- **Missouri - Jefferson City**
  Thomas Jefferson, holding a kitty (Kitty = City,) while
  riding a missile (Missile = Missouri.)

- **Montana - Helena**
  Helen Hunt, climbing a mountain. (Helen = Helena.
  Mountain = Montana.)

- **Nebraska - Lincoln**
  Remember how my wife said I should keep some
  images to myself? This image is Abraham Lincoln's
  statue sitting on my toilet, because that's where
  Nebraska falls in my Memory Palace. The statue has
  huge brass knees. (Lincoln = Lincoln. Brass Knees =
  Nebraska.) Lincoln looks like he's going to take a while.

- **Nevada - Carson City**
  This is a Car, sitting in the sun, with an unfortunate
  kitty (Carson City) inside. The car is parked outside a
  casino. Arguably, I could have saved the kitty, and
  pictured the car outside the Kitty Ranch I've heard
  about. The issues with that are 1) I don't know what the
  ranch looks like, 2) I don't want to google it to find out,
  and 3) I probably don't need that image in my head
  anyway.

- **New Hampshire - Concord**
  Two Hamsters (New Hampshire) flying the Concorde.
  In my image, the Concorde is half jet, and half bird.

- **New Jersey - Trenton**
  A tent is pitched in my image. (Tent = Trenton.) Out of
  it walks somebody wearing a football jersey that's so
  clean, it has to be a new jersey.

- **New Mexico - Santa Fe**
  Santa Claus (Santa = Santa Fe. Also, did I mention I
  love Christmas?) is dancing around a sombrero.
  (Sombrero = New Mexico.) In the first image I
  constructed, I pictured Santa eating at a Mexican
  restaurant I used to frequent. The problem was, I kept
  saying that this was Santa Fe, Stomach Pain. And that's
  not a state I want to be in.

- **New York - Albany**
  Tourists are taking pictures of the Statue of Liberty.
  (Statue of Liberty = New York.) The Statue has a
  puzzled look on her face, because the tourists are all
  bunnies. (All bunnies = Albany.)

- **North Carolina - Raleigh**
  Fortunately, Chicago is not the capital of Illinois.
  Otherwise this image might confuse me. (Side-note, I'm
  writing this from Chicago O'Hare airport.) I just see
  Michael Jordan (who played for North Carolina)
  dribbling a basketball. If you don't automatically know
  like I do, that Raleigh is NC's capital, then google Sir
  Walter Raleigh. Better yet, imagine Carolina
  cheerleaders, chanting, "Rah, Rah, Rah."

- **North Dakota - Bismarck**
  Dakota Fanning, is throwing a coat on a candy cane pole. (Candy Cane Pole = North Pole. Add that to Dakota and you get North Dakota.) She misses the mark, and the coat lands on the ground. (Missed Mark = Bismarck.)

- **Ohio - Columbus**
  Native Americans are on the shore, welcoming Christopher Columbus' ship. When they realize who he is, they say, "Oh, hi!" (Oh hi = Ohio.)

- **Oklahoma - Oklahoma City**
  No help here. I see my elementary school, which was Oakley Elementary, along with the stray cat from the school that we took home when I was a kid. (Oakley = Oklahoma. Cat = Kitty = City.) Try imagining the same cat stuck in an oak tree. The car was orange, and we named it, "Cat," because why give something a clever name if it doesn't come when you call it?

- **Oregon - Salem**
  A witch is cackling, as she plays a pipe organ. (Witch = Witch trials = Salem. Organ = Oregon. It has to be a pipe organ too, because otherwise, what's the point?)

- **Pennsylvania - Harrisburg**
  Remember Harry and the Henderson's? He was a lovable big foot monster. I picture a pencil (Pencil = Pennsylvania) drawing Harry, eating a hamburger. (Harry and burger = Harrisburg.)

- **Rhode Island - Providence**
  There's an old Michael W. Smith song called "Hand of Providence." That gets me to Providence. This picture is in my Palace's other bathroom, almost like it was meant to be. A tiny Michael W. Smith is singing the song, while floating on a tiny island (Island = Rhode Island) inside my toilet.

- **South Carolina - Columbia**
  I used to drive through Columbia quite often. One of the exits off I-26 that I remember vividly is exit 108, because there's a Cracker Barrel there. I picture the exit number. It only occurs to me just now, that I could probably have pictured a Cracker Barrel even easier.

- **South Dakota - Pierre**
  Dakota Fanning is back. She's sitting down, which means she's south of her former position. She happens to be sitting on a Pier labeled E. (Pier E = Pierre.)

- **Tennessee - Nashville**
  I visited the Grand Ole Opry a few times growing up. It's in Nashville, Tennessee. I met Grandpa Jones, and regretted not meeting Minnie Pearl. This image is Minnie Pearl, throwing open the door to my daughter's room, and waking her up by yelling her classic, "Hoooooowwwdyyyy!"

- **Texas - Austin**
  I played a lot of pickup basketball a few years back with a teenager named Austin. He threw up big bricks, the size of Texas, at the basket. (Not literal bricks, though he does in this image.) If you played basketball with us back then, this image will be perfect for you. (Hi, Austin. I really hope you're not reading this right now. But if you are, you know it's true.)

- **Utah - Salt Lake City**
  A lake of salt (Salt lake City) has a salt boat (whatever that is) making constant u-turns in it. (U-turn = Utah.)

- **Vermont - Montpelier**
  This one was hard. I rejected Mrs. Jones' suggestion for it, until I couldn't come up with anything better. It's an image of a mountain of fur (Fur Mount = Vermont) being peeled off (Mountain Peeled = Montpelier.)

- **Virginia - Richmond**
  This one is so unhelpful, it's barely worth explaining. And that's coming from the writer that just suggested you could remember Austin, Texas if you happened to have played basketball with him years ago. For both Virginia and West Virginia, I simply picture driving through the areas. Use the website again for help on these. For Virginia, it suggests a girl named Virginia, dating a man so rich, money is falling out of his pockets. (Virginia = Virginia. Rich man = Richmond.)

- **Washington - Olympia**
  George Washington is performing the pole vault at the Olympia. I mean, at the Olympics.

- **West Virginia - Charleston**
  The same girl from before named Virginia is now wearing a vest (Vest = West) and dancing the Charleston.

- **Wisconsin - Madison**
  My mom is scolding me. She is mad at her son, (Mad at son = Madison) for eating all the cheese. And also probably for that joke I made in the first part of this book. If she ever comes across it. (Cheese = Wisconsin.)

- **Wyoming - Cheyenne**
  A man is acting very shy. (Shy man = Cheyenne.) He is waving his hands as if to say, "No." And everyone knows that "Wyoming" is an old Native American word that means, "No State Here." Think about it. Have you ever met anyone from Wyoming? In all my travels, I haven't. (Hi Tony. I hope you're not reading this either. If you are, you should know that I stole your Wyoming joke years ago.)
  There. All 50 States and their capitals. Enjoy.

The only thing left now is to go back to what started this path of memorization for me.

Remember? What ever happened to solving the cube blindfolded?

I'm going to spare you the details behind how to solve a Rubik's cube. That's a different book altogether, and probably not one that should be written by me. As of this writing, my fastest timed solve took place in 41.73 seconds. That's a time sure to impress and amaze my friends. It's also a time that would make real speedcubers laugh, if I'm lucky, behind my back.

Yes. But solving it blindfolded. Did I ever manage it? Sort of.

I've solved it blindfolded several times, but I still often end up having four or more pieces out of place. Taking the time away from blind solving to write this book slowed my progress.

Addictive personality, remember? I'll get there consistently eventually. I thought the hard part was memorizing the cube. Turns out, the hard part was learning to memorize it without getting distracted by all the doors memorization opened up.

A theme of this book has been making memorization methods that work for you. As such, the way I learned to memorize the cube's colors might be instructive. Surely somebody uses a similar method to remember the cube, but I never came across it.

The method I decided to use is called Old Pochmann. It's impossible to switch a side or an edge on a cube without changing the positions or orientations of other pieces. Other methods for quickly solving the cube while looking at it switch too many pieces while solving. It's improbable to keep track of how they're all being changed without sight.

I say improbable instead of impossible, because the record for memorizing the most digits of pi is somewhere past 80,000. And no, I do not hold that record. I doubt I could get past 10,000. Heh.

Old Pochmann uses what's called a buffer piece. The positions of each of the edges and corners, in the order they will be solved. Then, in that same order, each piece is moved to the buffer, then inserted into its proper place. The next piece to solve is the last one replaced. Once the end of the memorized pieces list is reached, the cube is solved.

The first problem was I couldn't stand the way most people memorized the cube.

All the real cubers are about to roll their collective eyes at me. That's fine. They should feel free to go write their own book on memorization.

For the rest of you, consider this. Many cubers assign a letter to each sticker of their cube. The Blue-Yellow-Red corner piece might have an assignment of B-J-M respectively. The Yellow-Red side might be labeled as A-M. Then, based on those letters from the various pieces, they make images. For example, CL = Clown. BG = Bluegrass. So they see those corresponding cubes, and remember a clown playing Bluegrass music.

There's a small number of algorithms to learn in order to do Old Pochmann's method. It will take me less than a day to learn them, probably as soon as this book is finished. That's the blessing and the curse of this addictive personality. One fascination leads to another, which apparently sometimes leads to books.

I would like to suggest a better method for remembering the cube colors. First off, I use the body Memory Palace to place the images in.

My system has preassigned images for the colors. Green-White is the Hulk. Orientation of the colors matters, so I need a separate image for White-Green. That gets assigned to Mark Ruffalo, who played Bruce Banner, who turns into the Hulk.

The corner pieces have three colors. I use the same images for them, but I have an action associated with whichever color is on top (Or on the bottom, for the bottom of the cube.) Blue = crying. Green = stealing, because of green jealousy. Yellow = screaming, in yellow fear. White = Praying. Red = Pitching a temper tantrum. Finally, Orange = Setting something on fire.

This leads to images like Spider-Man setting my head on fire (Orange-Red-Blue,) or a Dragon screaming, "Run away," on my shoulder (Blue-Green-Orange.)

What's next for me? Consistently solving the cube blindfolded. Then I'm moving on to memorizing multiple decks of cards.

What's next for you? Tell me in a review, or by tweeting me at @thewritescott

Appendix: Resources

Fascinating, isn't it? Almost makes you want to read this entire book again. Who wouldn't? After that, consider looking into other resources as well. Here's a few to get started with.

- *http://artofmemory.com*
  A great place to start, especially for the forums. It also has a memory wiki.

- http://mrsjonesroom.com/themes/usa.html
  This is the site I used to construct many of my images for the 50 states. The order is laid out geographically.

- *Moonwalking With Einstein* by Joshua Foer
  Less instructive than many memory books, but it's so much more thoughtful. Nearly every recommended reading list on memory, post 2011 when Foer published it, has listed this book. That's probably what's going to happen to my book post 2016.
  Moonwalking is one of the better reads out there. Foer went from researching an article on the USA Memory Championships, to becoming a champion himself. This is his story.

- *Name Memory* by Ron White
  If you look up "Ron White + Names" and find something that says, "They Call Me Tater Salad," be aware that you've found the wrong Ron.
  The name method I use is largely (almost entirely) based off of the method described in this e-book. Over

60% of the book is dedicated to mnemonic suggestions for common names. (Contrast that to this book, where not even 60% of my name chapter was dedicated to suggestions.) If you find yourself struggling to figure out images for names, that's worth the cost alone.

- *How to Develop a Brilliant Memory Week By Week, 50 Proven Ways To Enhance Your Memory* by Dominic O'Brien
  Another book by another memory champion. You can bet that if I ever decide to compete, and actually manage to win a championship, I'll be writing another book about it.
  This one is exactly what it sounds like. It takes the reader through various ways to utilize the memory. For instance, Dominic developed the Dominic method mentioned in this book. He discusses that here. This book also demonstrates that a book title doesn't have to be short.

- *How To Learn & Memorize A Randomized Deck Of Cards* by Anthony Metivier
  Even though I used a different method than the one in this book, this is where I learned how easy it could be. Anthony also has books on vocabulary, with instructions on how to quickly learn new languages.

- *Magic Square* by Lewis Smile
  I thought this book would include instruction on memory techniques. It does not. However, it does teach a really cool math trick that you can perform, just by remember a handful of numbers.

- *Memory Palace, Remember Anything and Everything* by Think like Sherlock
  That's odd. I didn't realize until writing this appendix,

that this author uses a pseudonym. Either that, or he/she was given a really fortunate name at birth. The book goes into more detail about the Memory Palace.

- *Already Seen* by Scott Hughey
  Okay. This book doesn't have anything to do with memory, but if Nathan had known about these memory techniques when he gained the ability to reset time, his life would have been so much easier.
  Think about it. You can jump back in time, but you erase any notes or memos you've taken. How do you remember things?
  Check it here out today:
  https://www.amazon.com/Already-Seen-Scott-Hughey-ebook/dp/B00T82VEO2

Join My Reader List For Freebies

I hope you enjoy this story as much as I did writing it. If so, why not leave an Amazon review to help others find it? You can do so here.

http://amzn.to/2icnaRr

And also, be sure to sign up for my reader's group at

www.TheWriteScott.com

Members receive free stories for signing up, and get notified about upcoming books.

About the Author

Scott is an IT professional. You could change that today by purchasing a million copies of his work.

Printed in Great Britain
by Amazon